P9-EJI-654

THE
FRUITFUL
CITY

GIFT OF
FRIENDS OF
KENSINGTON LIBRARY

THE FRUITFUL CITY

THE ENDURING POWER OF THE URBAN FOOD FOREST

HELENA MONCRIEFF

WITHDRAWN

FRANCESCO'S FIG

Francesco's fig tree is on life support.

It squats behind a pale stuccoed house on a corner lot in Toronto's St. Clair West. It owns the space. No room to swing a bat or toss a ball here. The tree tucks in tight to a brick garage, stubby trunk shooting out sturdy branches that billow above the roof.

Decades ago, this Toronto neighbourhood drew European immigrants moving beyond their countrymen's first stop in the city's original Little Italy, a few kilometres south. It had slightly larger houses with room for a bigger garden — a step closer to settling in, away from the identity of newcomer. When I visit on a July morning, the tree looks lush with life, onion-shaped orbs of fruit showing the first blushes of aubergine on pale green. This most natural of conditions, a fruit tree bearing fruit, has taken a lot of human intervention.

Every fall for the past 20 years, before the frost set in, Francesco and the men of the neighbourhood sweated together to bind the tree branches upward. They lassoed the giant, pulling ropes toward the trunk until it stood rigid. They covered it in layers of plastic and tarps and more ropes. It took an afternoon of struggle followed by homemade grappa, shared after a good job done, glasses held in calloused hands.

Fig trees need heat. Canada doesn't have much of that. So men like Francesco, immigrants determined to make the New World their own, improvise. Some dig trenches as long as their trees are high and, also with the help of friends, grab hold of the trunk and rock the tree back and forth, patiently watching until the root ball is loose enough to tip the well-wrapped plant into a temporary grave. Francesco, with a tree grown tall and a small yard, didn't have room for that. So he improvised again. Deep inside the shrouds, he set four cinder blocks around the trunk, building a tiny room for the tree's base. He dropped a line of plastic piping into the centre, teepee-like to let the moisture escape. Then, to ensure the tree would survive another winter, he installed a thermostat and a space heater.

This fig tree is known in the neighbourhood as "the mother." Francesco had been generous in sharing not only the bounty of the honey-dripping fruit, but cuttings from the tree. Her offspring are in yards and sunrooms many blocks from her home off the back stoop of Francesco's house.

Last winter, Francesco died. His family packed up his belongings, his shovels and rakes and pruning shears, and prepared the house for sale, doing their best to showcase the curb appeal by removing the rows and rows of plumber's pipe that held up grapevines and beans. His son didn't have the heart to turn off the heat on the fig tree, so she lived on to see one more spring.

The new owners, a couple with young children, hadn't considered the burden of the legacy and now are faced with a decision: provide perpetual care or pull the plug.

Francesco's tree was the source of much more than fruit. It was a private tree, the yard fenced off from interlopers, but I'd learn that Francesco was generous with his harvests. He'd share fruit and vegetables, and he involved his neighbours and friends in his garden. It was the source of a lot of sidewalk conversations, providing a summer equivalent to the introductions that snow shovelling makes on a stormy winter evening. He turned on many passersby to city-grown fruit they wouldn't have tried otherwise, and he showed them that a local garden can make a difference in how we think about food, farming and the health of the planet.

Laura Reinsborough introduced me to the fig tree and the little orchard within earshot of the city's streetcars. Laura is the founder of Toronto's urban harvest program, Not Far From The Tree. It's the country's largest in a burgeoning field of not-for-profit city fruit-picking outfits. The model is simple: volunteers clear out unwanted fruit from backyards and share the bounty among the homeowner, the pickers and organizations that help people in need of food.

As she was wrapping up her tenure at Not Far From The Tree in 2015, Laura took me on a tour of the neighbourhood around Not Far From The Tree's headquarters. It was also her home territory and ground zero for her career as a community builder, which came about through a late-blooming connection to urban fruit trees. We walked through laneways behind the shops of

St. Clair Avenue, a paint store, dry cleaner, animal hospital, small restaurants and nail salons. She encouraged me to peek over the back fences protecting the private homes that back on to the commercial strip. The hoardings offer homeowners and tenants privacy from the recycling bins, parked cars and windswept jumbles of newspapers and empty coffee cups. On the other side of weathered wood, chain-link or latticework, she pointed out cherry and apple trees. Some she knew, others she had her eye on for future seasons. On a May afternoon they were promises of the bounty to come. Overgrown, mostly, but a big part of each yard's allure as a green oasis in the middle of the city — wooden Muskoka chairs and a hammock in one, a green plastic turtle sandbox in another. I imagined swinging in that hammock on a lazy Saturday, reaching up and picking cherries without having to put down the book I'd be reading. On the day of our walk, schools were still in session; the yards were deserted. We popped out of the lane and headed north across St. Clair, Laura offering to show me something "very special."

Up one street and down another she had a memory of each fruit tree her team had picked and others that she was watching. I had seen Laura's TEDx talk about her project. She strode into the spotlight and pointed to a projected screen image of downtown skyscrapers and the CN Tower. "I live in an orchard," she told the audience. "It looks like a city, but I kid you not, it is an orchard." As we continued our tour, Laura showing me how to identify the trees by their bark and shape and which streets were more likely to have crabapples or cherries, I started to see things her way.

We headed back toward St. Clair and slowed down as we approached a barn-shaped house in pale beige stucco. "OK, so here's the property," she said. She had walked past this house for years and knew the friendly man who shared his fruits. A few weeks earlier, Not Far From The Tree had a message from someone requesting help with their newly purchased home and its 12 fruit trees. Laura recognized the address. It was Francesco's house.

The house had been sold, and the new owners had moved in, all before the growing season had started again.

It did have a lot of fruit trees, carefully pruned to keep the fruits in reach for picking. I could see that there wasn't much room for anything else. It wouldn't be a place to have a barbecue in the summer. Laura had gone with a crew to check it out. "We don't actually do site visits in advance, but I felt like this was a part of me getting closure on the project and also us being able to get 12 trees," she said.

We walked along the sidewalk looking through the chain-link fence that marks the perimeter. "I hope they don't mind if we take a little look," she said. She told me that in her brief reconnaissance visit several people had come by asking what had happened to the man who had cared for the trees. When home ownership changes, it's an adjustment for the whole neighbourhood. Can you still walk across the grass? Are you still sharing tools? Who shovels the shared driveway? Perhaps the new owners don't want to be on display all the time.

I looked at the trees and guessed at what they might be, based on bark, leaves and Laura's notes from our tour. Apple, cherry, apricot, plum. "And that," Laura said, pointing to the patch between the back stoop and garage, "is the fig tree." We both stopped, silent for a moment. I thought about how much had gone on around that tree over the years. Laura had told me Francesco would call out to passersby, including her.

"I got the full Italian treatment, the '*Mangia, mangia.*' He brought over a fig right off the tree still warm from the sun. That was my first fresh fig. I thought figs were like Fig Newtons, that was it. But to have one so warm from the sun, ripe right off of the tree . . .

"And so this beautiful corner lot has been sold to new owners and what to do? What to do with these 12 fruit trees?" She didn't have an answer to the new owners' dilemma.

The high buzz of a jet overhead broke the spell, and Laura asked if we could take a double selfie. We'd connected a lot over her past year with the organization, as I chronicled the work and its meaning. It happened to be her farewell tour, and she was assessing the impact, considering what she had built. Heads together, we grinned into her phone as Justine Shiell-Cappel stepped out the back door, a toddler on her hip. She waved a hello.

"We were just talking about how it might well be a

burden for you to consider how to carry on the legacy," Laura called out.

"Yeah, it is. It looks like they're getting close, some of them," Justine said, referring to the ripeness of the crop. "You can come in if you want."

I did want to go in, but we were all on school pick-up time. I tossed a question over the fence instead. "Are you planning on keeping them, or are you feeling pressure?"

"Yeah, both. I think my husband wants to see what's healthy this summer and then get a sense of what to keep. It's also an expensive proposition to start pulling out trees right now, so we'll see how it goes."

Her husband, Aaron Cappel, joined in, loading a stroller: "Also, we actually like the fruit."

"Yeah, there's that," Justine responded. "The fig tree I don't think we intend to maintain after this season."

Aaron and Justine moved into their new home in the spring. They had been looking for more space for their growing family and had a list of must-haves and nice-to-haves. An orchard wasn't one of them.

I sat down with Aaron in their sunroom (it was crammed with plants and trees when they first saw the place) on a July morning in the peak of fruit season. I stepped over apricots rolling on the sidewalk on my way to the door. They were spotted, but I was pretty sure they'd be salvageable for cooking or smoothies. With the help of an arborist, Aaron had identified the diseased branches and trees, had them pruned and had taken out an ailing apple, planted too close to the house, and the grapevines. Neighbourhood reaction was mixed. "It's so interesting," Aaron starts. "The old people, some of them really love what this guy did with his yard, and many of them really hated it because they thought it was an eyesore. It was too much."

When we were arranging to meet, two older women with limited English were half pleading, half scolding, "Not to cut, eat. Very good." They pointed to the fig.

Clearly, this tree was part of the community. People were counting on it. It may have been a sentimental notion to honour the work that went into nurturing the fig for so long, or it may have been a desire to maintain the source of those delicious morsels. But the fig was a private tree. No vote would be required to decide its fate.

Aaron is a slim man, a musician and elementary school music teacher. Although it's hardly a desk job, his work doesn't involve routine heavy lifting. As Aaron worked on pulling out the apple trunk, the 80-year-old man across the street trimming his manicured hedge and lawn noticed and came to help. "He doesn't speak really any English and he tried to communicate that it was messy, and he started helping me with a spade and getting the roots out and he was better than me at it," Aaron laughs.

Justine, he says, had a better grasp of what was involved,

how much work would be ahead. They decided to see what came in the first season: "Let's see what we actually like eating before we make any major decisions about what we're going to keep and not keep," Aaron says.

Aaron was home for the summer with more time to explore, research and share the discoveries with his toddler son. His daughter had already taken ownership of the bounty, cross at people picking the cherries overhanging the sidewalk. Through the season, I watched the decisions take shape. The apple tree in front of the house was first to go. An apricot tree disappeared a few weeks after its fruit had fallen. The fig was a tougher call. Aaron and Justine had been going by trial and error trying to figure out the ripeness. And they felt the pressure from family and others who wanted to try the showcase fruit.

"So we've eaten a few that are ripe and they're really good. I've never had a fresh fig before. There's something a little weird about them, they're kind of like a different texture than anything else I've ever tasted, they're kind of gross a little bit, like gooey . . ."

As the summer wore on, Aaron and his family had to decide what to do with the fig. The season ended, the leaves began to fall. I drove past in September and October, en route from our youngest daughter's school. Still no wrapping. By early November, after heavy rains and wind, the trees were bare and the fig was uncovered. The final days, I thought. Over lunch one Monday afternoon, I listened to *Ontario Today*, a CBC Radio program;

that day's show included a segment with gardener Ed Lawrence. Lawrence was the chief horticultural specialist to six governors general, tending their official grounds in Ottawa. Listeners call in to talk about their plant woes. On this day, a woman's voice came through the phone lines talking about a fig tree. I put down my sandwich to hear her story. She said she had moved into a new home in the winter, in Toronto, near Bathurst and St. Clair. She had a fig tree that had been heated through the winter. It had to be Justine. She said she had loved the fresh figs and wanted advice on how to cover it for the winter.

In 2011, our eldest daughter, Gwendolyn, added Not Far From The Tree to her high school volunteer hours roster, and for several summers had filled our kitchen with bags of free fruit and stories from the trees. This is my home-town; I thought I knew what it had to offer, so I was stunned to see how much fruit was growing and going for free. I was horrified when I realized that but for this band of volunteer pickers, it would all go to waste.

Yet these trees are really just the tip of the landfill; massive waste is the collateral damage of our industrial food system. While parents once chastised children for not cleaning their plates when there were starving people in [insert any country suffering from famine here], now the shame is heaped on corporations in the food industry that toss out misshapen or bruised produce. The Food and Agriculture Organization of the United Nations estimates that, each year, approximately one-third of all food produced in the world for human consumption is lost or wasted. That equals 1.3 billion tonnes of food a year wasted on the farm, in processing, transportation, restaurants, grocery stores and by consumers. Value Chain Management International looked specifically at the fruit chain and found that of 100 tonnes of fruit grown, just 63.5 tons is purchased. The losses occur all along the chain, from harvesting and packing to distributing and retailing. We're all responsible. From a business perspective, if consumers won't buy it, why try to sell it? We value uniformity; we question aberrations, even in food.

With so much food already being squandered, it is easy to feel that a little tree in a backyard won't matter to world hunger, depletion of resources and the growth of landfills. But reducing waste, I was about to find out, is not the only reason for picking fruit in a neighbour's backyard.

The word "locavore" is a creation of the 21st century. Eating local has become a lofty pursuit, imbuing those who can do it exclusively with the prestige that might have gone to the connoisseur of the fifties who could source the best Russian caviar, find strawberries in February or sneak a fresh pineapple in from Hawaii. Sometimes there are political reasons for drawing a geographic border around our plates, but more commonly today, it's an environmental and nutritional concern. Restaurants and grocery stores highlight locally produced vegetables and meats, equating local with fresh and assurances that knowledge of where the food is grown somehow makes it safer. Defining "local" is a matter of opinion for most of us. The Canadian government expanded its definition in 2013 when it moved from food originating within 50 kilometres of where it is sold to food produced in the same province or territory or 50 kilometres from the border. So as interest in eating local grew, so did the definition of what makes something local. At the same time, the idea of hyper-local — eating fruit grown in sight of your own kitchen window, perhaps — is still met with a degree of trepidation by those who aren't seasoned gardeners or foragers.

At some point we knew how to identify which plants would nourish us and which could be used as poisons. As our parents and grandparents turned their backs on homegrown food in favour of the convenience of industrialized supplies (and who could blame them when they were still hand-wringing laundry), many of us lost the generational knowledge that should have been passed on as routinely as shoelace tying. I felt stupid when I didn't recognize the mulberries and serviceberries Gwendolyn lugged through the door, and asked, like so many others have, "Are they safe to eat?"

Yet it's not too late to turn things around. Laura's organization and more than a dozen others across Canada are leading the fruit-picking renaissance; they've also popped up in the United States and beyond. It's a wedge into new efforts to reclaim not just the fruit, but the knowledge of and connection with food. Nurseries are seeing an uptick in fruiting plant sales, although nowhere near what they once were. Connon Nurseries, for example, has been growing, wholesaling and retailing plants in Ontario for more than a century. Sales manager Brad Hale says the new interest has more to do with the experience, the desire for freshness and the knowledge gained from growing food yourself than with the economic imperative it once was.

Even if viewers don't head to the kitchen, having an entire television network devoted to food, at minimum, shows an interest in how food can be prepared. A Neilsen Global Ingredients survey released in 2016 found that 80 percent of Canadians believe food prepared at home is healthier and look for products without artificial ingredients. Farmers' markets are increasingly popular, with more than 600 operating in Canada and more than 8,600 registered in the U.S., almost double the number from 10 years ago. These phenomena are all clues to a new fascination with what we've lost. A growth in allotment gardens and urban agriculture shows the interest in action. A not-for-profit called the Bowery Project, for example, started in 2014, turning vacant spaces into temporary places to grow food using easily movable milk crate planters. The produce goes to local chefs and charities. Many schools across the country have added food-producing gardens to their greenspace; some are able to turn the small farms into cafeteria fare or, in partnership with outside organizations, student employment.

All of these efforts are worthwhile. But my fixation on fruit trees comes from their longevity. Backyard tomatoes, fava beans, kale and lettuce have to be replanted each year. When the urban farmer moves away, or loses interest, the garden plot can quickly return to wild plants and weeds, with little trace of what was once there. The fruit trees endure, the agricultural equivalent of tagging, leaving markers across our cities of who came before and a taste of what they ate.

When Gwendolyn left for university in Halifax, I signed on to pick, armed with sunscreen, gardening gloves and a lot of questions. How old were the trees and who had planted them? Who wouldn't pick fruit from a tree in their own backyard? When did we stop seeing the usefulness of a homegrown tree? How can we have food banks and soup kitchens campaigning for more when this bounty exists in neighbourhoods across the country?

Soon I was talking to fruit tree planters and pickers, canners and chefs, historians and home economists. I set out to eat, pick and visit more trees across the country and talk to the people who had figured out what the city fruit tree has to offer in the 21st century.

WRAPPED FIGS (GLUTEN-FREE)

Francesco Vaccaro's family ate figs the best way: fresh from the tree. For a fancier treat, they dressed them with prosciutto and balsamic vinegar cream glaze.

INGREDIENTS

Balsamic vinegar
Fresh figs, sliced in half
Prosciutto slices

INSTRUCTIONS

1. *Pour one cup of balsamic vinegar into a small saucepan. For a sweeter flavour, add a tablespoon of honey or maple syrup to the pot. Bring to a boil, then reduce heat to allow vinegar to simmer. Stir occasionally until liquid is reduced and thickened (about 10 minutes).*

2. *Drizzle the vinegar glaze over the prosciutto slices. Roll a half fig in each piece. Hold in place with a toothpick, if required.*

CHAPTER ONE

PUTTING DOWN ROOTS

IMMIGRANTS ARRIVE BEARING FRUIT

Francesco isn't the first man to carry fruit from his homeland to a new world. He's not even the first to do so successfully against tremendous odds. With the exception of berries and other very small fruits, most of what we put on our tables in Canada originates from somewhere else. Plums, pears, peaches and even the lunch bag staple sweet apple are not native to this country. Explorers, settlers and immigrants carried seeds and shoots for grafting across oceans to satisfy their cravings. In the process, they shaped the landscape and culinary tastes of their new home.

In our age of convenience, with grocery stores overflowing with fruits, it would be easy to ask "Why bother?" Most of us don't bother today. But the few who do are driven. It seems to be part of our nature as humans, perhaps connected to a natural fear of hunger and starvation, to carry our own food. And even when we don't need that homegrown delicacy, desire takes over. In a paper about food and the immigrant experience, Mustafa Koç and Jennifer Walsh say, "'Feeling at home' is not simply limited to having access to a nutritionally sufficient diet, but also to culturally appropriate foods." Koç has spent his academic career studying food security and the sociology of migration. He's a founder of the Centre for Studies in Food Security, Food Secure Canada and the Association for Food Studies. Jennifer Walsh was his colleague at Toronto's Ryerson University, on a campus beside one of Canada's busiest intersections. Among Ryerson's buildings is the former Maple Leaf Gardens, steps from the Eaton Centre, the neon signs of Yonge Street and concerts at Dundas Square. More than 860,000 pedestrians pass through Yonge and Dundas every day. They come from all over the world. In their paper, "Food, Foodways and Immigrant Experience," Koç and Walsh say, "If we learn and define who we are through what we eat, the multicultural cuisine may offer a glimpse of widening notions of identity, self and belonging in Canada." Something as simple as figs from Italy could be a part of this cuisine. They point to research carried out in Toronto with newcomers from Algeria, Zaire, Somalia and Vietnam. "Freshness was a recurring theme . . . a longing for the tastier and fresher fruits and vegetables of their home country . . ."

Travel by streetcar in Toronto and you'll see hints of the ethnic makeup of each neighbourhood by the language on the storefronts. Walk through the city and you get another look at the natural landscape. A glimpse down an alleyway or over a backyard fence offers clues about who came before, who not only lived on this land but lived off of it.

Toronto was far from ground zero for the first immigrant fruits to Canada. The founder of New France, Samuel de Champlain planted apples in Quebec early in the 1600s. So did his compatriot Louis Hébert, who is said to have been the first settler in Canada to live off the land. It's believed that settlers in Port Royal had apple trees growing by 1610. Certainly, the people of Nova Scotia's

Annapolis Royal, as it's now known, would consider their region as one of the original fruit belts. The Mi'kmaq in the area had been doing just fine for thousands of years without the need for apples beyond the wild sour crabs. I wonder what they thought of the foreign produce. These new people sailing across the ocean arrived with an interest in fur trading and planted small gardens and apple trees around the trading posts. Had they been able to carry them on their ships, grafts of French apple branches would have given the settlers fruit they could eat. More likely, they brought seeds that produce terrible-tasting fruit, suitable only for cider — at least until pollination with other trees, and combinations of rootstock and grafting, developed more palatable fruit. No matter: the fermented beverage provided a safe alternative to water full of bacteria.

In *Voyages de Samuel de Champlain*, the geographer's vivid recounting of his explorations, Champlain describes the trial of the group's first full winter in 1605. Snow and ice kept them from finding food and crossing the river. "We were obliged to drink very bad water, and drink melted snow, as there were no springs nor brooks." They didn't have enough food and couldn't get enough sleep. They ate salt-cured meat and vegetables, the latter, Champlain was convinced, the cause of bad blood. He wasn't alone in his thinking. It was commonly believed at the time that vegetables were unhealthy foods. "During this winter, all our liquors froze, except the Spanish wine [today's sherry]. Cider was dispensed by the pound." Imagine cracking through frozen cider to get your daily allotment. The vitamin C may be what saved the few who survived.

I've found no record of what kind of apples they brought. I imagine the names didn't matter. More importantly, they carried varieties that could withstand the cold winters and flourish. Whether it was by chance or design we may never know. We spend a lot of time identifying and labelling fruits now, certain that we can differentiate between an Empire and a Cortland. I wonder if their palates were so refined and if they could taste the difference between an apple grown in the New World and one grown in French soil.

The apple plantings survived and caught on. Another explorer, Étienne Brûlé, travelled up the St. Lawrence River and into Lake Ontario in 1610. He was followed a few years later by Champlain. More fruits arrived. And so did women. Within a few decades, one in seven rural Quebec households kept an apple or plum orchard. It's said that some French women refused to stop in Quebec because the climate wouldn't support peaches. They carried on on Brûlé's path, many landing in Niagara. Jesuit pear trees are considered living evidence of French settlements in the Detroit/Windsor area. Some still fruit two hundred years on.

On a 1719 map from the Ontario archives, pale, watery colours of pink, green and yellow mark off sections of the geography, and cartographer Henri Chatelain had covered the margins in tidy script with lists of fruits and other resources identified around what we now know as Ontario. He documented apples, pears, plums, cherries and a variety of nut trees "*comme en Europe*." Four berry species are listed too: strawberries, raspberries, blueberries and currants.

In fact, more than two hundred small fruits are native to Canada. That might sound like plenty, but most don't appear in our pantries. To call them all berries is a simplification, although that's what they look like. Blueberries and gooseberries are "true berries." The rest fall into the categories of drupes, like cherries and elderberries; pomes, such as saskatoons or serviceberries, as they are known in the East; and aggregates, like strawberries and raspberries. They've grown here for a long time. Indigenous people used silver buffaloberries to flavour, as the name suggests, buffalo meat. Saskatoons were a key ingredient in pemmican. Plenty more of those native fruits are said to be tart but very good in jellies. You could survive on them if you were lost in the woods, but most need a lot of sugar to make them truly palatable to today's tastes.

The Huron-Wendat tapped maple trees, harvested berries and grew corn, beans and squash in small clearings in what's now Southern Ontario. The habitat was rich with wildlife, horticulture, shelter and access to water travel for many Indigenous societies. A short article in *First Nations House* magazine on Toronto's

Indigenous history describes the area as being not unlike the Mediterranean, "in that many cultures and peoples met for the purposes of trade and commerce — dating back thousands of years prior to European contact."

In the 1790s, Elizabeth Simcoe, wife of the first lieutenant-governor of Upper Canada, John Graves Simcoe, wrote in her diary about the berries she collected — fox berries, mountain tea berries and wild gooseberries that, she reported, were excellent stewed as sauce for salmon. The Mohawks gave her young son Francis a gift of cranberries, and Francis offered apples in return. At their white pine cabin on the edge of the Don River, young Francis, whose ailments are well documented in the diary, was said to be "much better, and busy in planting currant bushes and peach trees." The peach tree is long gone, and all that's left of the estate is a subway station name, its nomenclature taken from the cabin aspirationally dubbed in honour of the son: Castle Frank.

Mrs. Simcoe wrote plenty about the Indigenous visitors and the exchanges of goods between them. We might see them as the equivalent of today's hostess gifts, but they were eminently practical in the 18th century. A trip to Niagara in the heat of July prompted observations about how welcome the fruits were.

We treated them with cherries. The Indians are particularly fond of fruit. We have thirty large May Duke cherry trees behind the house, and

three standard peach trees, which supplied us
last autumn for tarts and desserts during six
weeks, besides the numbers the young men eat.
My share was trifling compared with theirs, and
I eat thirty in a day. They were very small and
high flavoured. When tired of eating them raw,
Mr. Talbot roasted them, and they were very good.

By the 1800s, Toronto was dotted with orchards, planted by British immigrants who came to farm and set up new estates. The apples were as important to them as they were to Champlain and his party. They couldn't have imagined that something they worked so hard to establish would be discounted as useless mess by their descendants.

In late summer I join a lost rivers and orchards tour in Toronto. I was looking for evidence of the foreign fruit trees that had shaped our urban landscape. As a child of immigrants, the history of my own place here doesn't go back further than my parents' experiences. My mother arrived from Scotland in the late 1920s, and my father from Ireland in the late 1940s. From our dinner table discussions, any history before that took us across an ocean to another world. Many of the city's trees, including the fruit-bearers, predate my family's arrival. So I tie up my shoes and travel four subway stops east to learn more. The tour was put on by Lost Rivers, an organization working to encourage an understanding of the city as part of nature. We've really messed with our natural surroundings here, so it sounds like a finger-in-the-dyke goal. Still, I like the idea of paying homage to what came before the sandblasted renos, paved roads, cars and millions of people in a 630-square-kilometre space.

A dozen of us meet on the corner of a popular city park across from a mall teeming with traffic. I try to envision the place as it was: trees, a creek and more trees. Although we're a few kilometres away from the site of the Simcoes' retreat on the Don River, I can picture the space as Elizabeth sketched her estate. Thick trees reach down to the water, cleared in places for roads and houses, but still plenty of wild land for gathering all of those berries. Toronto's Parks, Forestry and Recreation Division markets its vision of Toronto as "a city within a park." It's an apt description. The city does have greenspace, although arguably not enough, and few of us get to the riverbanks and ravines that hold the last pockets of wilderness. Led by Helen Mills, our group of mostly women will weave through the long-gone Garrison Creek. Kitted out with a straw hat tied beneath her chin, Helen has spent a lot of volunteer hours looking at the history of her second home. Hints of her South African heritage slip into her voice as she tells us we are standing on a buried creek. The water flowed where we now see a trough of ravines running through this part of the city. "Whose bright idea was that to cover the river?" one of our group asks. Helen explains that as the population grew, the creek was overused as a sewer. It was also the source of drinking water. As public health concepts developed in the early 1900s, the creek was buried to help combat typhus and other diseases.

Our other guide, Becky Thomas from Not Far From The Tree, turns us from thoughts of sewage and disease to the orchards that would have edged the creek. The orchards have fewer lasting markers. Historical documents and maps are the only means of tracking where they were. A slight woman, soft-spoken with an open smile, Becky points to a large tree at our meeting place. It's a black walnut, she tells us, absolutely edible but really difficult to crack. I pick up a shell from the ground. A squirrel, most likely, has gnawed through and eaten the meat. Deep grooves mark the dark brown cover; split open, it looks skeletal. I put it in my pocket. I've never tasted one and now I'm curious. The Society for Ontario Nut Growers says the black walnut is highly valued for its timber and, because it can stand the cold, is one of the most successful edible nut trees in the province. Indigenous people ate the nuts raw or pounded them into a butter. Early pioneers valued the rich flavour and also used the hulls to produce hair and fabric dye. A craft studio not far from our tour route offers two-day natural dye workshops for $125. When the much-easier-to-crack Persian or English walnuts arrived in our grocery stores after the

1930s, most took the path of least resistance. As I stand fingering the thick shell in my pocket, I remember when bowls of nuts appeared on the coffee table at Christmas. Cracking walnuts was great entertainment for my siblings and me. An uncle had us entranced when he cracked the English walnuts with his bare hands. That was something to aspire to.

We head down the street and stop at a white mulberry tree outside a corner house. Helen tells us about the 1900s attempt to bring the silk industry here. Silkworms love mulberry leaves. So the trees had to come first. The silk industry didn't work, but the trees endured and spread, crossbreeding with the indigenous red mulberry. The red mulberry is now an endangered species, with the imported whites the biggest threat. Helen pulls a package of dried fruit from her bag just as a young guy pulls up on a bike. He stops fast, a heavy metal chain swinging from his neck. White sunglasses cover his eyes under spiked bleached hair. We are snapped out of the Edwardian Age. He lives in this house and has no idea what the tree is but knows that the birds seem to like it. He wants to hear everything. "This is awesome," he says. "I love you guys." We sample the dried mulberries. I've seen them in the bulk stores packaged at almost $10 a bag. They are much sweeter than the fresh fruit, almost like candy. I think about investing in a dryer. Helen and Becky tell us about the difference between red and white mulberries and where they can be found. "You know those things that just happen in your day?" the bike dude interjects, still in awe at the anachronistic information he's hearing. He's coming back to the present. "I'd stay, but the NFL calls." He shrugs, grinning, and rolls his bike up to the house.

The tour continues and Becky stops us at a ginkgo tree. It's not part of a lost orchard, but it produces fruit and it's a tree of note. The ginkgo is considered a living fossil because it has remained unchanged (the only member of its genus, family and order) since before the time of the dinosaurs. Becky asks if we know why the females aren't planted much anymore. I can't stop myself from blurting out the obvious. "They stink."

"It's a combination of diaper and vomit," offers another in our group.

I tell everyone how I spent weeks one fall scraping down my daughters' shoes at lunchtime, convinced one of us had stepped in dog poop. Yes, but inside, Becky insists, if you scrape the fruit off the nuts and roast them, they are a delicacy. "They're really nice," she smiles, head cocked. Another in our tour agrees, suggesting the best way to cook them. "Fried in butter, everything fried in butter . . ."

We move on through Old Orchard Public School's yard, connected with a grassy field, a garden and a small stand of apple trees, a nod, we're told, to the school's namesake. I've seen the name, read the name and said "Old Orchard" countless times. It shows up on street signs, parks and neighbourhoods not just here but in many parts of the city. But I hadn't thought of the logical connection between the name and the one-time existence of an actual orchard. In New York, I went to Mulberry Street looking for early signs of the trees — I found crabapples instead. But I had let the names remain places in my own city. The students at this school won't do the same. Paper cups held up with pipe cleaners hang from branches. Whether they are an art project or a means to keep the wasps away, the trees and their place in this neighbourhood have been worked into the curriculum. I pick an apple and have a few bites. It's not the best specimen — hard, with lines of rust inside.

There were orchards everywhere in this neighbourhood, it seems, none of the fruit native to the area. By the 1800s, settlers were growing 79 different varieties of apples here — golden pippins, June sweetings and russets. As the travellers moved farther along the lakes and rivers, so did the fruit.

Architect John Howard and his wife, Jemima, arrived from England in 1832. Their cottage on a hill overlooking Lake Ontario is now a city museum, restored to a moment in time. Howard left the cottage and property to the city for use as parkland with a lot of restrictions that block development, one of the best gifts ever, to my mind. I grew up at the north end of High Park and moved back to the same area as an adult. It's been a playground, a source of science and exploration, a retreat from the heat and noise of the city, and a place simply to be. On one of many strolls through the park I stopped in at the lodge. A swish of skirts preceded Catherine Raven, a historical interpreter, dressed in period costume. She took me to the back porch, birdcage undergarment swinging as she pulled a black shawl around her shoulders. In early spring with grey skies, walking through a chilled bare-floored house, I was transported back 180 years and imagined the kitchen garden just outside the window. Raven described Howard's apples, plums, peaches and quince. His diaries talk of distribution to anyone in need and about selling fruit to the local store. It was part business for him and part challenge. "He would have been in his potting shed, with a paintbrush, sexing plants," Raven told me. He had to crossbreed varieties from England to make them able to withstand the cold.

Just a single cherry tree has survived, now wizened and barren. The rest were lost to blight. The trees could be replaced with hardier breeds, but the rules of the museum won't allow that. Too bad. Howard was trying to do the same thing.

We continue our Toronto tour, looking and listening for more clues of the city as natural pantry. We see dips in the landscape, reminders of buried waterways, the odd out-of-place apple tree, perhaps a descendant from a dropped core. We can't know for sure. What we do know is that immigrants continued to come to Canada and to this city. Chinese people had been in Canada from 1788, but arrived in larger numbers during the gold rush and then again during the construction of the Canadian Pacific Railway in the 1880s. The hostile restrictions on their citizenship were such that the ability to own city property and plant gardens was limited. Culinary historian Shirley Lum notes that there wasn't time or money to care for a tree, and little point in planting a tree that would take years to fruit when you were moving often. So, although we see vegetable gardens in the yards of Chinese-Canadian homes, there are few enduring markers of agriculture. New waves did operate farms in British Columbia, with entire families engaged in supplying grocery stores with produce. In the 1890s, cabinet minister Clifford Sifton was keen on populating the Prairies with agricultural immigrants. "I think that a stalwart peasant in a sheepskin coat, born to the soil, whose forefathers have been farmers for ten generations, with a stout wife and half-dozen children, is good quality," he wrote. The farmers came, many of them Ukrainian, settling the West on free homesteads. But cities also became magnets for newcomers with a longing to put their hands in the earth and familiar food on their tables. A second wave of immigrants from Eastern Europe and the Baltic States and elsewhere fleeing oppression came much later. They carried just the essentials, with no option for going back to bring favourite fruits.

In a study published in the *Journal of Arboriculture* in 2000, Evan Fraser and Andrew Kenney, both University of Toronto foresters, found three distinct landscape histories in the city: "the British landscape tradition, which is dominated both economically and culturally by large forests, the Mediterranean, which emulates small-scale agriculture, and the Chinese, which has evolved a tradition of abstract ornamental gardens."

With a team of interviewers, they talked to Torontonians of each ethnic origin, asking about their preferences for landscape. The British chose big shade trees like oaks, a practice, Fraser and Kenney say, with origins in the Middle Ages, when the elite provided land for hunting. "Forested manor homes became a symbol of wealth, power and prestige of upper-class society," they wrote. The Chinese, influenced by the relationship between Confucianism and Taoism and who would have had little say in shaping cities, continued to see the private courtyard as the outdoor space. But for the past three thousand years the design of that space has had more to do with water, stone and abstractions of nature than with big trees and lawns. The fruit trees I've been tracking outside of this Lost Rivers tour are clearly the work of the Italians and Portuguese. A long history of intensive small-scale agriculture left little wild or natural land in their home countries. The foresters summarized the work of J. Houston in *The Western Mediterranean World*. The Mediterranean landscape culture, they wrote, is "a conflict between fruitfulness and frugality, where nothing but ingenuity allowed people to harvest rich crops from soil degraded by millennia of use."

Fraser and Kenney concluded, "Being one of the earliest hubs of Western society, the Mediterranean has undergone a vast transformation over the centuries. Much of the original landscape and native vegetation have been lost for centuries and largely replaced by agricultural and introduced species. A naturalized landscape, which is the goal of some contemporary North American greenspace planning, may seem foreign to people coming from a land where the natural landscape vanished centuries ago."

In a follow-up question in Fraser and Kenney's work, the study subjects were asked what kind of tree they had or would plant. The Brits would go with shade trees, the Chinese didn't want any trees and the Italians and Portuguese would choose a fruit tree.

With that research in mind, I look at the neighbours in my city a bit differently. We are all shaping the landscape to suit what we think feels like home, our own version of natural.

The travellers kept coming, each group bringing something new. In addition to the apples and plums, they introduced cherries, peaches and apricots. When large numbers of post–World War II migrants from Italy, Greece and Portugal chose city life in Canada, orchards moved to often-small backyards, and for the most-devoted pomiculturists, they included the labour-intensive figs.

Neighbours lent a hand in the lifting and shovelling. Everyone had an opinion on when and how to prune. And when harvest time came, the bounty was shared among multiple families and often passersby. Everyone had a stake in their success; everyone became part of a new community.

We stop at a small house to meet a fellow who's offered to tour us through his front yard orchard. We follow Helen's straw hat through the gate and see about half a dozen short trees on a lot that would barely fit a car. The practice of converting front yards into parking pads has been suspended in the city. This yard is a good example of how much can come out of a small space, whether it's food, gardens that feed the butterflies and bees or air-scrubbing trees. Gabriel is waiting for us. Plaid flannel shirt, charcoal trousers held up with suspenders, keys dangling at the back. His tanned face is shadowed by a weathered black ball cap. His daughter excuses herself through the crowd to get to his side, leaning in to ask a question in Portuguese. "I guess I'm here to translate," she says. She tells us about a special tree, a red plum, planted close to the front door. "That came from Portugal," she says. "In Madeira my father had a lot of fruit trees. When he came to this country he wanted the same." He started buying plants from local nurseries, she tells us, but couldn't find the bigger red plum he craved from home, so he grafted a branch onto a local tree. I have to interrupt. "How did you get the branch here?" There is a long pause through the translation; Gabriel's shoulders lift in a shrug, palms turning upward. He sends his left fingers up his right sleeve, then mimes lifting a suitcase. I don't need to understand Portuguese to figure out what he is describing. He had slipped the precious branches, cuttings from a tree back home, into the sleeves of a jacket, then carefully packed them into his luggage. I'm curious about how the cuttings made the trip. Gabriel motions up to the sky. "Colder," he says. "Cut at night, next day no problem."

Father and daughter shift, turning their gaze elsewhere. The topic of smuggled fruit and cuttings quiets many old-school gardeners in this time of increased border vigilance.

Our fig man, Francesco Vaccaro, was born in Calabria, the toe of Italy's boot. Hot and dry in summer and mild in winter, it has the perfect environment for growing fruit. Olives, lemons, oranges and figs need no coddling there. Francesco was born on a farm during the Great Depression, when tensions were building to war; it was a tough time in the poorest part of the country. His family raised live-stock and grew olives. Francesco became an expert pruner, supplementing his income as a labourer on construction projects. By the '70s, although the rest of the country had seen some economic improvements, the South hadn't ben-efitted and poverty continued to push people away, looking for opportunities to earn. Francesco left his wife and four children behind, boarded an airplane and went in search of a better life in Canada. His third son, Natale, was six when Francesco sent for the family to start their new life. Nat joins me for coffee near his house in Etobicoke to fill in the details on his father's little orchard.

When the family arrived at their new home, the yard

was a blank curve of grass, popular in the '70s. That didn't last long. Francesco planted fruit trees and vegetables and herbs. More than an orchard, Nat remembers it as a forest. It was a source of food but also embarrassment. It was a reminder to the prepubescent kid that his family was different simply by planting fruits and vegetables in the front yard instead of in the back. "It doesn't look nice when you put all these fruit trees or you plant tomatoes on the side," he remembers advising his father. "It's not nice. People will make fun of us."

I think of how many schoolyard fights start with kids feeling the sting of not fitting in. Young Nat had bigger worries when it came time to fertilize the garden. "It wasn't like now. You didn't go to Loblaws. You went to the farm where there were cows and you picked up cow manure. You put it in bushels and bags and you took that home. And I was like, 'Dad, you know it's disgusting, it's whatever. It's embarrassing. I don't want to do this.' I was 10 years old and I'm like, 'What if my friends see me and I'm picking up shit?'" he lowers his voice, his dark eyes checking the room, as if it still has to be a secret, then breaks into a laugh, runs his hand across his closely shaved head. "That's the way it was.

"My father said, 'This is my property . . . If I'm going to pay taxes on the property here, I'm gonna cultivate it. I'm going to grow our own stuff. I want to eat stuff that's organic, I want to eat stuff that I know . . . I don't put pesticides, I don't put chemicals, I know what I eat.'"

He was not alone being so adamant in his need for natural produce. And yet in the '70s we might have equated that more with the natural food stores, then staffed by long-haired, unshaven, patchouli-oil-scented 20-year-olds, than with a construction worker from Calabria. He also had a low carbon footprint, functioning without a car or driver's licence.

Nat's father had tried earlier to grow a few fig trees without success — they couldn't take the cold. This one, though, the mother, took. Until she grew too tall, she was buried each fall and revived each spring. Her heritage is a bit murky.

"I think he smuggled a branch. He cut a little small clipping and he put it in a zip-lock bag and so he used that when he came back to graft those trees with the figs from Italy."

"Are all of those trees somehow connected?"

"Some were, but others were probably from other immigrants, other family members who had given cuttings and then he'd graft. So most of his trees there, they didn't come from Home Depot. He'd pick a wild tree — it could be an apple tree — he would graft it and make it his own."

Nat mimes the technique, each hand movement precise with meaning: peeling the bark, cutting to a thin slip, inserting, binding with rags and string, watching for the eye to sprout.

There was, and still is, a lot of trading going on. You taste or see something you like and make a deal. I give you a clipping from an Italian plum, you give me a clipping from a Bing cherry. And when your fellow deal maker has also slipped favourites in from the homeland, the trees get interesting.

"So these trees could be part Sicilian, part Calabrese," I say.

"Exactly. You know my dad had friends from all walks of life — Portuguese, Spanish, Greeks. He had a best friend; I think his name was Nick. And he actually gave him a couple of clippings that he had brought from Greece a few years ago and he had grafted on that fig tree as well."

Francesco wrapped and buried that tree until it grew too large, then he built the heating system. He gave his hunting dog, Gena, a heated doghouse too. She lived outside beside the tree, two treasures side by side. The wrapping task was at least a two-man job. Nat remembers the ritual, but he was never the second pair of hands.

Neighbours, friends and hunting buddies joined in. It was hard work, but an event.

"He never asked you to help?"

"No. It was something they did together. It was like an accomplishment. Wow, look at the season that it had. 'Cause he would share. He shared those figs with the neighbour Mike, with the neighbour that gave him the figs from Greece, with somebody else that would help him, so it was a way of giving to each other so they helped him and they ate from them; they were there for all to be had."

Weeks before Francesco died, Nat, in his forties, had

one more opportunity. "So that year, he's got cancer, he can hardly walk, his bones are brittle, he's in pain," Nat crosses his arms on the table, wincing with the memory. He joined his dad and a neighbour in the burial task. They pulled on the ropes, Francesco up the ladder until Nat couldn't bear to watch. He convinced his father to let him take his place.

"I looked at the neighbour helping us that year. I go, 'Mike, you know what, my dad . . .'" Nat has to stop for a moment. "He knew. My neighbour knew but my dad didn't know. I said he's going to be gone, the fig tree is still going to be here. Look at the irony. He's so passionate about this fig tree and he's going to catch pneumonia out here."

Francesco did get sick a short time later. He was coughing and second-guessing his decision to sacrifice his energy on the tree. Nat shrugs it off as another illustration of the passion his father had for the fig.

It was not, however, a passion held by the women in the lives of men like Francesco. The figs were shared immediately, not stored to sustain a family through our frigid winters. It's a fruit best eaten soon after picking. It doesn't ripen off the tree. And it takes a lot of work for a relatively small yield.

Nat laughs as his thoughts turn to his mother's views on working for 15 figs in some years. He channels her emotion: "'What are you doing this for? For 15 figs you can go to the store and buy them.'" His fingers are pinched together, emphasizing the point. "'You don't have to kill yourself doing all this work.' And my dad was like, 'Yeah, but they're not mine.'

"He could have been tending to us, spending time with us, but he was more into tending the fruit trees. It was a lot of work."

His mom would have preferred a patio, would have surrendered year-round to the store-bought fruits they ate through the winter. She had full-time jobs as well, working at a dry cleaner or as a restaurant cook. She took care of four kids. She'd come home at the end of the day to Francesco waiting for dinner, to more cooking, laundry and then what she saw as the chore of cleaning up the fallen cherries and leaves. Where her husband wanted to eat organic, her view was, Nat recalls, turning his palms upward, "You're going to die anyways."

In the novel *Kicking the Sky*, Anthony De Sa writes from his childhood growing up in Toronto's Portuguese community around the same time as Francesco was setting down his roots. I met Anthony in the spring sitting outside a bookshop with a group of writers supporting independent bookstores in the city. He had brought Portuguese custard tarts to share with his fellow authors as they chatted with customers, fans and readers about literature and storytelling.

In the novel, the fictional Antonio is unable to stomach a backyard pig slaughter, a significant event for the men of the community. As the story nears its end, the 12-year-old finally has his coming-of-age experience around a fig tree.

"Antonio!" my father yelled from two backyards over. He stood beside my uncles, who were in the middle of lifting the fig from its sleeping hole. "Ajuda! We need one more man."

The passage is vivid with detail on the coils of rope around the men's wrists, the call of *"um, dos, três,"* the pink insulation and newspaper stuffed among the branches, the dust and the dirt.

Like Nat, four kilometres to the north, Anthony never actually helped out.

"That never happened in real life. I'm a fiction writer. But as a boy I always wanted to do that," Anthony told me. "The truth is, when I got to the age where I could help them, I wasn't interested. I was going through that, you know, I didn't want to have anything to do with being Portuguese. All of that stuff was kind of silly and so I missed it. Sadly, I missed it. But I appreciate it now tremendously."

Anthony pulled out his cell and showed me pictures of his uncle David's yard. In one photo, David stood with his arm curved around a 49-year-old grapevine that must have been 10 inches in diameter. It towered over his head, crawling along metal piping built up like scaffolding across his small backyard lot. A worn chain-link fence surrounded the lot, ladders hung from the sides of faded blue metal hoarding sheets, and black tarps covered structures behind him. His uncle stood looking bemused, plaid shirt sleeves rolled up to his elbows. I guessed he was in the middle of spring cleanup when Anthony captured the image. Small sprouts of green poked through a patch of soil close to the house over his right shoulder.

Anthony thumbed the screen, scrolling to an image of the fig tree, just starting to bud, leaves not yet out but tiny pimples of green fruit already forming. The tree was surrounded by orange plastic fencing, the kind you see on construction sites. It was held up by two-by-fours crossed at either end, sealed up to keep the squirrels out.

I asked about the provenance of the tree. I was quickly learning that the idea of heading to a nursery and buying seemed to be an unlikely scenario for this particular generation of urban gardener.

"So, we always grew up with the idea . . . they won't tell us one way or the other that these things were brought over from Portugal."

In those days, the '60s and '70s, security at airports wasn't what it is today. Passengers descended the airplane steps onto the tarmac, and family could watch from the airport windows. Anthony remembered the excitement of picking up an aunt or uncle who had travelled to Portugal in the summer. He knew their bags would contain all sorts of interesting things. "I still remember as a child getting into my grandmother's kitchen and having my uncle open up his bag and having live crabs come out of the bag! And there was another bag with sausage and cheese and then there was tucked in an area of the bag, there were paper towels that had been moistened and carefully layered with plastic and plastic bags and in it were seeds; what would you call them, cuttings?"

They were cuttings from grapevines, and the hope was that they could get them growing and plant them here. So much of what we see in the backyards in some of our neighbourhoods came from those places.

"And did they take?"

Anthony seemed as amazed today as he would have been then. "Yes!"

So the hints that the figs came from Portugal are probably close to the truth. Anthony suspects the goal wasn't to feed a family, no more than the rock crabs were, but to provide a link to home. "I think for them it had a lot of symbolic meaning about the place they came from, the place they left behind and I think it was almost a link to that place for them, which I really think is almost more beautiful than the practical thing of getting fruit and feeding your family."

It also wasn't about the taste. "It was the fact that we could do it. I was listening to an interview recently about how we've really moved away from the '50s and '60s in terms of how remarkable that time was in our world history because it was a time when people did things because they just wanted to. They wanted to go to the moon. Why? Because we can. And that spirit is gone. And I think that's really exciting that that was part of it as well. It's not really about the fruit; it's about 'let's see if we can.'"

It was a challenge for these men. Anthony points out that there was no fear of weather where they came from. In Portugal, the fear was of the power of the sea. Winter and the cold was an unknown foe to conquer. They took it on, adding to the Canadian literary theme of man against nature. "I think that really is the magical part of and such a metaphor for what it is to survive in this country as an immigrant," Anthony said. "It's to find ways to make things flourish in sometimes a very inhospitable kind of place, a foreign place, a strange place."

Laura Reinsborough and her team of volunteers started tracking fruit from the beginning of the project. They made notes on where they found fruit trees and how much they picked. They set up a database organized by the city's municipal electoral boundaries and applied it to a city map. Just like any of us zooming in on Google Earth, I looked at my own neighbourhood. Ninety-four trees were registered in 2016, the largest proportion of them cherries. It's not the only area with cherries topping the charts, but I was curious about why that would be so in an Eastern European neighbourhood. It's also the riding that houses High Park's ornamental cherry blossoms. I wondered if the two were confused.

The area was a popular landing spot for Ukrainians from the 1950s on. Many were fleeing economic and political instability; some came as defectors from the Communist bloc. Of course neighbourhoods change, but Ukrainian is still spoken on the street, and roads are blocked off each fall for the Ukrainian Festival. These trees are old enough to have been planted by those newcomers in the '50s and '60s. I remember a friend's grandfather making us cherry pierogis (*varenyky*) as an after-school snack. I asked my old classmates about what was in their backyards. Perhaps their parents or babas had a hand in the planting.

The answer came from a colleague, Vera Beletzan. Over a faculty lunch, she told me she'd been to Ukrainian school. When I asked about the significance of cherry trees, she started to recite a poem. "*Sadok vyshnevyi kolo khaty* . . . A cherry orchard by the house / Above the cherries beetles hum . . ."

She told me every Ukrainian school kid knows, or did know, that Taras Shevchenko poem. Shevchenko is considered the founder of modern Ukrainian literature. Born a serf, then orphaned, he was a servant, and when his artistic skill was discovered he was contracted out to paint. A group of noted writers and artists raised money to buy his freedom in 1838.

The Shevchenko museum is a short walk from my home. I popped in and met Lyudmyla Pogoryelova, the museum's director. As we wandered through the few rooms of displays, looking at portraits and artwork of the man with the dark eyes and furrowed brows, she talked about his unfortunate life, the growth of his political activity and his arrest by Tsarist Russian police. His punishment for agitating for the end of serfdom was 25 years of military exile, and worse. "They took away what was most important to him," Lyudmyla said. He was forbidden to write or paint.

We climbed the stairs to the museum's small library. Lyudmyla hunted the shelves for a particular edition of *Kobzar*, Shevchenko's ongoing book of poetry. It was no bigger than most cellphones, a reproduction of Shevchenko's original in handwritten Cyrillic script. We turned to the orchard poem, and Lyudmyla said it was among the pieces written during the poet's exile. She gestured to her shoe: despite the risk, he hid a small pencil and paper in his boot.

The poem stands out among his works because it is light, romantic. "Sadness is like a red line throughout his poetry," the director said. He missed his family, he missed his country and then he became political, advocating for freedom. His work was sad, yet prophetic. When the situation is difficult in Ukraine, as it has been over the years, Lyudmyla insists you just have to open his poetry and read. "This is a book of old recipes. Many pieces of his poetry tell us what to do. We just have to follow."

The cherry tree was and still is part of the idyllic view of Ukrainian village life. Cherry trees show up in many of the paintings in the museum beside white houses with thatched roofs, families eating and sleeping outside. "It's very calm, and very lovely, a typical summer day for them," Lyudmyla said.

"Is it true?" I asked, wondering if it was an unattainable ideal for everyone.

"Yes it is."

"Just not for him?"

"He missed it very much, but he did not have it."

The image endures, and the idea of having that cherry tree, of walking under blossoms is powerful enough to make Gabriel, Francesco and all the Old World gardeners find a way, against the odds, to make something grow where it ought not.

These recipes come from *The Common Sense Recipe Book:*
Containing All the Latest Recipes on Cooking with Economy
and Also Very Valuable Medicinal Recipes, published by John
Lovell & Son in Montreal in 1895. They offer a clue to the
scant details required for many home cooks of the day.

APPLE SHORTCAKE

Season apple sauce with butter, sugar, etc.; make a nice
shortcake, open and butter it and put the apple sauce in layers.
Serve with sweetened cream.

CENTENNIAL APPLE PIE

Peel one dozen and a half of good apples, take out the cores,
cut them small, put into a stew pan that will just hold them
with a little water, a little cinnamon, two cloves, the rind of
a lemon; stew over a slow fire until quite soft, then sweeten
them, pass it through a hair sieve, add the yolks of four eggs
and one white, quarter of a pound of good butter, half a
nutmeg, the peel of a lemon grated, and the juice of one
lemon; beat all well together, line the inside of the pie dish
with good puff paste, put in the pie, and bake half an hour.

CHAPTER TWO

PLANTING SEEDS

THE VICTORIA FRUIT TREE PROJECT

Matthew Kemshaw steps inside the warehouse refrigerator at Victoria's LifeCycles' new headquarters. Transport-truck big, the concrete space is near empty save for a wall of orange industrial shelving and a few bundles on the floor. I slip into my jacket and breathe in the stale smell of onions and old greens.

"There's so much we can do with this," Matthew says, heading toward a collection of mismatched cardboard boxes overstuffed with robust-looking Bosc and Bartlett pears.

A previous tenant would have filled this space with carefully packaged produce: cartons of carrots, washed and bagged; peaches, brushed, washed and air-dried then boxed in single layers; crates of pears, swaddled in protective tissue paper to shield them from pressure changes and bumps. Ripe soft fruit doesn't travel well, as many of us have discovered from finding a puddle of sweet nectar in the bottom of a picnic basket. It also doesn't last long, so spaces like this are way stations, refrigeration slowing down the ripening process but not completely stopping it. While some apples can last through the winter in cold storage, in Canada, there had been no such luck with pears. That changed in 2015 when the Cold Snap pear debuted at the Royal Agricultural Winter Fair. Enthusiastic ambassadors staffing a booth offered slices of the wonder fruit. From the hype of something new in a shiny plastic bag designed to look like a frosty winter window, I expected to taste a flavour wow. In fact, it tasted like a pear, as it should. The then-called Harovin Sundown was developed by Agriculture and Agri-Food Canada researchers in Harrow, Ontario, part of Canada's most southern region. Scientists bred the variety to resist fire blight and to have a longer storage life.

Getting the pears from the trees into those glossy blue bags takes a lot of steps for commercial growers. The fruit has to be picked green at just the right firmness. Orchard farmers use a penetrometer, a syringe-like device that measures the pounds per square inch of firmness. They plunge an 8 mm diameter tip into the pears for a scaled reading to ensure the fruit is at just the right point for picking. Farmers in California have been trying optical density measurements using multiple wavelength light transmittance meters. They're also measuring chlorophyll content using near-infrared spectrometry.

The fruit in LifeCycles' warehouse was tested with fingers and teeth. It came from Victoria's backyards, picked by volunteers with LifeCycles' Victoria Fruit Tree Project. Homeowners would have taken a bite and declared the fruit ready or close enough to pick. Collectively, they've brought fruit back to its simplest: grow, pick, eat. We can do this; the fruit is OK to eat, even without all of the high-tech gadgets of the commercial world.

The project harvested forty-two thousand pounds of fruit in 2015; it was a national-record year of picking city fruit that would have gone unused. Instead, a portion went to community organizations, some went to the pickers and homeowners and the rest was added to fundraising ventures that make up 10 percent of the Fruit Tree Project's budget. We step back into the front office, unairconditioned in the August heat, and Matthew points in the direction of an independent wine store down the road where I can purchase a growler of the project's Backyard Blend cider. Profits from the brewer-made beverage are shared with the Fruit Tree Project. In the fall, a few grocery stores sell quince paste made in partnership with a local chef or by volunteers working out of a rented kitchen. Area food processors who don't mind a few spots on their apples pick up city-grown fruit from this warehouse to turn into juice, pies and sauces. A gelato maker has been among LifeCycles' clients. Matthew turns to his laptop and with a few keystrokes notes that the outfit also gleaned eight thousand pounds of produce from local farmers who had finished harvesting. Because it's farm food, he's able to parse out the value: $23,000. The value of the backyard food is tougher to quantify.

Among Matthew's interests, as the organization's seed library manager, is ensuring a local source of food by sharing what grows well in the area. There aren't many BC seed producers and none in the city of Victoria. Instead, the library enables backyard cultivars that may be family heirlooms passed from European grandmothers to daughters to grandsons to get back into public circulation. Another community-led program, GRAFT, Growing Regionally

Adapted Fruit Trees, is part of the work of a Ph.D. candidate. Organizers have been collecting scion wood from all over the region and teaching people how to graft. Leaning back, Matthew mentions the Welland Legacy Orchard. It's a public orchard left to the community by conservationist Rex Welland, who had filled his backyard with a collection of diverse apple trees, one hundred of them rare heritage varieties. LifeCycles stepped in to help care for the site. "We've been doing a lot of place-based education there and teaching people how to graft and grafting some of the real rare trees." So it's not just about food. These living museum pieces bridge old Victoria with its Coast Salish and British heritage today.

The Victoria Fruit Tree Project has come a long way over the decades. In another part of town, across the blue-hued Johnson Street Bridge, past the tour buses and high teas of Government Street, Lee Herrin meets me at the hip Cornerstone Cafe. It's a social enterprise in support of Fernwood Neighbourhood Resource Group, or Fernwood NRG, as it's known. In 1998, Lee and Matt Strand created the Victoria Fruit Tree Project, the first urban harvest outfit of its kind in Canada and, as far as I can tell, in North America. Not all organizations hang a shingle, electronic or otherwise. No doubt individuals have been picking and sharing for a very long time, but the formal structure with overall goals and a set ratio for distributing the fruit started here in Victoria.

Lee is executive director of Fernwood NRG, a driving

force behind community cleanup and support. He greets the barista and many others in the café by name and offers me anything I'd like. We sit close to the cash, close to the screech of the milk frother. Lee, with his back to the wall, can see everyone coming and going from this spot. He steps away to speak with people at another table. In this space, he's the man.

In the late '80s, Lee was a long-haired, overall-wearing student at the University of Victoria. Money was tight, so when he noticed bushels of fruit falling to the ground from a neighbour's apple tree, he knocked on the door hoping to trade his brawn for fruit. It didn't go well.

At the time, Lee didn't understand what an elderly woman's thoughts might be upon seeing a scruffy-looking teen on her doorstep asking if he could pick fruit from her tree. He walked away angry. Now, head shaved, dressed in a grey vest over a button-down shirt, a more mature Lee still has a tinge of annoyance in his voice as he recalls that time. "You know, over the next three months I watched hundreds of pounds of fruit rot and I knew what I was paying for that in the store. I just felt it was a waste."

That feeling was inspirational. He had spent his summers with the family of a girlfriend, pressing apples into cider at a Saturday market in Duncan, in the southeast of Vancouver Island. Food and nature were setting his path. Lee finished his degree in English and philosophy, then moved to Toronto for graduate school and a focus on rural sustainability. He called his major project We Exuberant

Ones, using "exuberant" from the Latin, meaning fruitful. He was, he says, "fully steeped in fruit." When he headed back to Victoria with a master's degree in environmental studies from York University, he was changed.

"So here I was in the fall, back in Victoria, walking through some of the suburban neighbourhoods and the urban parts of the city and everywhere I looked it was like 'Wow! There's a plum, there's a cherry, there's an apple, there's a pear.' And some of those trees were quite large and [had] just massive quantities dropping."

Within a month he had a plan. He took it to Matt, who was working with LifeCycles. The nonprofit had been running for about four years by then, cultivating community health by connecting people, food and land. Matt brought Lee's idea to the higher-ups.

"And they came back and said no," Lee says, still sounding disbelieving. "So I said to my friend, 'Let's do this anyways.'"

Lee and Matt's initiative put them about 20 years ahead of the curve on awareness of food waste. In 2015, Nesta, a UK charity that backs creative innovations, predicted that gleaning would change attitudes toward food waste. It pointed to the rise of gleaning organizations in the UK and around the world. The prognostication followed the European Commission's declaration of 2014 as the year against food waste. The commission encouraged people to look at what they buy and what they toss in the garbage, among other calls to action. In that year against food waste, retailers in several European countries introduced "ugly fruit," the misshapen produce that wouldn't usually show up on store shelves. Canadian grocers followed a year later, marketing imperfect fruits and vegetables as environment- and wallet-friendly options. In 2015, France went a step further with a new law that required large supermarkets to donate unsold food to charity or to have it used for animal feed or energy generation. It's an after-the-fact form of gleaning.

The concept isn't new. Gleaning shows up in the Bible as the practice of gathering leftover produce from harvests that would otherwise be left in the fields. Farmers, with loads of grain or vegetables, aren't going back for the bits and pieces missed or dropped from their carts. Today's urban gleaners are taking what would end up in brown paper leaf bags left at the curb.

Lee and Matt started work on a database. "We went to the market with a laminated lot map of the city and coloured pins," Lee starts. I reach Matt later; he's on vacation at a family property on Saturna Island, British Columbia. He fills in the details. "We'd ask people if they had a fruit tree and they'd put a pin in their lot matching the fruit — red for apples, purple for plums, green for pears," he says, remembering the image of the map. As the map filled with pins, interest grew. There was a lot of unused fruit hanging in the city.

They didn't have computers; registration was carried out on paper sign-up sheets, and the pair put up posters around town. A $15 fee for the farmers' market stall, $50 for a map, a corkboard, pins and some printed sheets from a home computer and they were in business. Although he was unemployed, Lee bankrolled the roughly $100 start-up.

The original brochure is pale yellow, a standard-sized page folded to create four panels. Lee still has a copy. On the cover panel a woodcut-style tree boasting overlarge fruit is encircled by the organization's newly minted appellation: the Victoria Fruit Tree Project. Underneath is the manifesto: "It is the ultimate goal of the Victoria Fruit Tree Project to generate a genuine understanding of both the heritage of our past and our duty to the future as represented by the beautiful, bountiful fruit trees of our fair city."

Lee put it together himself. "I had a bunch of hippie magazines and pulled these graphics out of there with my scanner and la la la."

I balk at the scanning. I've worked in some fields that have been quite competitive and sometimes adversarial — news and politics, for instance. But the nonprofits, I've learned, share a lot. In fact, Lee sees a value in open-source branding, using the same name for services offered around the world. So, for example, he'd like to see all urban harvesters called the Fruit Tree Project. Many of them in British Columbia have taken on the name — I mistakenly thought they were all connected — but elsewhere, creativity abounds, with monikers including Out of Your

Tree in Saskatoon, Fruit for All in Sudbury, Operation Fruit Rescue in Edmonton and Les Fruit Défendu in Montreal.

At a national gathering to discuss parks in 2015, that willingness to share freely was not only evident, but the point of the weekend. The Toronto Park Summit attracted about four hundred people that year, making it the largest gathering of park enthusiasts in Canada. Participants shared experiences, expertise and food in a slick series of presentations, including orchestrated PowerPoints, videos and panel discussions. It was open and free to anyone who wanted to attend. A fellow from one of several parks named "Orchard" told the audience how he was inspired by a cider festival he attended in the city, so he called up Not Far From The Tree (NFFTT) and asked if he could borrow the organization's fruit press to start a similar but small-scale event in his neighbourhood. NFFTT had never done that before but said yes. No charge. The point is to engage more people, to inspire more to do similar good work and to help people. For many social agencies, the highest goal is to not be needed anymore, for there to be no hunger, poverty or waste.

That's not to say there are no rivalries. Lee and others have butted heads on use of public space. He has strong feelings about the practicality of community efforts. We take a walk through Fernwood, Lee stopping to chat to women tending the vegetable garden outside a child-care centre, showing me where tomatoes, apples, lettuce, berries and other food has been planted in unusable spaces. He points to a new community orchard on a slope behind the building. The whir and bang of skateboarders tricking on makeshift ramps tamps down the birdsong. The trees are young; a few apples look good, but it will be years before they are ready to produce a pantry-filling harvest. Lee has visions of cooks using the fruit to supplement the childcare meals. The city has other ideas. Because it is public space, and parents pay a fee for the daycare spots, using the fruit turns that otherwise empty knoll at the edge of an asphalt playground into a commercial venture. Not allowed with public spaces. Lee sloughs off the objection with a harrumph, the absurdity of being prevented from picking fruit and using it to feed children too much for him to deal with.

We stroll farther, past quiet shaded homes, to the city's edible forest, Spring Ridge Common (or Commons — there is a heated language debate about this that has involved a war of plastic wood and carving tools as opponents furtively change the overhead wooden sign). Lee points out the medlar tree. Orangish, it looks like a small apple that's been chewed through the bottom by a ravenous squirrel. I wouldn't think to pick it. It's made palatable by a process called bletting. You store the fruits in a paper bag or box until they are wrinkled and soft. The result is a pulp reminiscent of spiced applesauce, according to the sign beside the tree. I've never tasted one.

Cultivated by ancient Persians and Greeks, the plant travelled and became popular in Victorian England.

Lee shakes his head at the choice. "If the ambition is for it to be a food forest, why don't we plant more things like apples and plums and pears that people recognize and will actually eat?" The larger question is which people? The area has its share of homeless and hungry. Certainly the recognizable trees with fruit that can be eaten immediately would be useful. But I see a large pear tree leaning over a fence into a nearby alleyway. This city does have a lot of accessible, although technically private, fruit. Horticulturally and gastronomically, there is merit in trying out something new. Lee, referring to the "food security fetishists," calls it an ideological miss.

I go back to Spring Ridge Common later, and Mary, who's been watering and digging throughout the morning, agrees to take a break and show me the highlights. The foliage is dense. I can't see from one side to the other, a telling exercise in how much can be done with an empty lot. Volunteers with a permaculture bent created the common in 1999 from a hard-packed gravel parking lot on the site of a former school. It sits on traditional Songhees territory, and Indigenous people practised early food forest management here, harvesting camas bulbs to roast and eat. The showy periwinkle purple camas lilies grow well in meadows around Garry oaks, the only native oak trees in Western Canada. Some Indigenous people burned woodlands and meadows to keep the land open and allow for berries, nuts and roots, including the camas bulbs, to grow. The same techniques are used today. Toronto's High Park smells like a campground for a day each year as foresters set prescribed burns to ensure the oak savannah, a similar ecological feature, continues. The oak trees can't grow in dense underbrush.

What once was wide-open terrain is now a short square city block in Victoria. A fence separates the common from two-storey homes to one side; roadways form the other three borders. Mary points to a peach tree, figs on their second fruiting (it's warm enough for figs here), cherries and plums finished for the season planted among the berry bushes and herbs. The miniature forest contains more than one hundred species of plants. In addition to the recognizable apples, saskatoons and raspberries, volunteers have planted ginkgo, black bamboo and cardoon, not quite household names. A young guy in baggy jeans sits on a bench in the middle of the space and pops open a beer. He doesn't reach for the grapes or the medlars nearby.

During the week of my visit, the provincial government, through a court injunction, shut down a large tent city in a municipal park next to a downtown courthouse. More than three hundred people were sent off, and with them their blue and green plastic tarps, shopping carts and the bits and pieces of life necessities that can fit into pockets and backpacks. The province moved them to shelters and other accommodations, pledging to create more affordable housing. Before the tent city was in full swing, the high bushes around Spring Ridge provided good shelters. Lee figures there were 15 to 20 campers around the neighbourhood, creating the detritus that results from having no washrooms, kitchens, closets or simply walls. The neighbours had had enough. They hacked back the bushes, cleaned up the garbage and opened up the space, making it less attractive for living. Not everyone was happy with the approach. Lee sees it as an example of working with the neighbourhood rather than sticking to an ideology. "I'm on the front line here . . . It's not just about whether the plants are arranged properly, it's about how it fits in the community."

Lee puts a lot of thought into what happens in this neighbourhood, how one effort affects another. In his early days as a new graduate, his approach was a little less fleshed out. Waste was one of Lee and Matt's motivations. The nut of their original project shows on an inside panel of the brochure. They described the Victoria Fruit Tree Project as a plan to capture as much as possible of the wasted fruit and sought permission to harvest fruit and pick up windfalls, and promised to leave the tree and the ground clean in exchange for a portion of the bounty.

"Those were the days," Lee says. He was 26 at the time, Matt a bit younger. "Just call me and Matt. I knew I was in trouble when I'd get home from drinking with my friends and I had like 10 calls. It was like, 'Oh shit, this is actually happening.'"

They didn't have a fully developed game plan for what to do with the share that was to go back to the project. Matt guffawed recalling the result, when I asked him about it during our phone call. He had use of a LifeCycles pickup truck — a baby blue '80s-era Ford, "barely functioning, gasping on its last legs." They filled it with apples and drove it to Cobble Hill, a small community north of Victoria. Lee knew a guy who had an apple press there. Matt remembers pressing apples well into the night, bottling the juice and then waiting for it to ferment. "We made a lot of apple cider and had many sudsy nights traipsing around Victoria living off the libations."

In the first year of the Victoria Fruit Tree Project, pickers harvested one ton of fruit, Lee tells me. The second year, he figured they might double that, but they quintupled it. "We hadn't thought through cold storage. In Victoria in the fall it can be quite warm still," Lee remembers. At that time he and Matt were living together in a house. They piled the bounty in the yard and on their porch. Pick after pick came in with nowhere to go. "It's one thing to say, 'Oh yeah, we're going to harvest this fruit and make sure it gets to good use.' It's another thing to have three tons of apples rotting on your front porch. And I'm not kidding. We couldn't get this stuff out fast enough."

Necessity is the mother of invention, as we know. With mounds of fruit attracting all manner of pests, they most definitely had a need. "OK, so you had this smart idea," Lee told himself. "Now what, genius? How are you going to move this?" They had to come up with a faster means of getting the fruit to the agencies in need of food. No more just figuring it out as they went along. They created a planning system to match the harvest with the food bank before the pick and ensured there was someone who could transport the food immediately. That cut out the waste. It may seem obvious today, but he cuts himself some slack. "We were trying something new. You could have potentially anticipated it, but you could have anticipated that people would have said, 'Forget it, we don't want some hippies coming to pick our fruit.'"

Ensuring there is someone to take the fruit is part of the model of many of the organizations across the country. In Toronto it can be a complicated formula. Not only does NFFTT need an agency willing to take sometimes one hundred pounds of fruit at a time, but that agency has to be reasonably close to the tree. With a zero carbon footprint commitment, the Toronto fruit travels only by cargo bike. I met a woman on my first serviceberry harvest who was trying to organize a team that could respond at any time to an unexpected arrival of fruit at a mental health agency where she worked. She planned to have recipes, jars, extra ingredients and trained volunteers at the ready to process large batches of fruit. I pictured a SWAT team armed with aprons and peelers, waiting for the call. Sometimes I could use a SWAT team of my own. I've had all kinds of fruit-enamoured flies in my kitchen because I haven't had the time to chop, simmer or can a large batch fast enough.

In Winnipeg, Fruit Share has taken itself out of the picking game. Instead, it's set up a portal called Fruit Connect for tree owners and pickers to connect online. In the Fruit Connect model, strangers trade sweat for fruit. It takes the labour costs of coordinating picks off Fruit Share's books, but the downside, founder Getty Stewart notes, is reduced engagement and a loss of feeling part of a community. Pickers may arrive over several hours or days, individually or in groups. There's not necessarily one big picking event per tree. While Fruit Connect encourages sharing the fruit with agencies in need, there is no guarantee of that happening and no organizational connection at the handover.

Lee's concept has been replicated in many cities over the past decade and a half, including Vancouver, Edmonton, Calgary, Saskatoon, Winnipeg, Toronto, Ottawa, Hamilton, Montreal, Halifax and many points in between. Village Harvest, working in the San Francisco Bay Area of California, keeps a partial list of several dozen American organizations that includes the Baltimore Orchard Project in the east to the Portland Fruit Tree Project in the west. Ripe Near Me in Adelaide, Australia, offers options to sell unwanted fruit, and Pick Your (City) Fruit in Lisbon, Portugal, focuses on creating and sharing public orchards. Ottawa's Hidden Harvest set up a listserv called Fruit Rollup that allows for some sharing of information. I've found no national or international umbrella group or complete online resource; so, there is no repository of the best techniques, resources available or even the history of the movement.

Ottawa's Katrina Siks, Winnipeg's Getty Stewart and Toronto's Laura Reinsborough and Sue Arndt held a workshop for aspiring gleaners at Food Secure Canada's 2016 assembly. It was a rare moment, catching them in conversation in the same room — Katrina tapped in via Skype. A younger Lee Herrin could have used her advice on the early days of urban harvesting. No one is lukewarm about using wasted food. Enthusiasm abounds. "Prepare for success," she advised those thinking about setting up an urban harvest organization. "Prepare for an onslaught of energy."

The social innovation of Lee and Matt was threefold. First, they organized the project. They brought it into existence. Lee remembers an introductory speech from the dean of graduate studies at York University. He said, "We need examples. Nothing in existence is impossible." It stuck with him. "I think that that is so often true in community development. Someone has an idea and someone else says, 'Oh that'll never work because blah, blah, blah.' If the person who has that shut down comes back and says, 'Well it's working in Victoria,' and can point at it, then nobody can say it's impossible."

So that was the first step, making it possible. The second element was figuring out the legal aspects. "If you just make a deal between neighbours, nobody is going to be too fussed about it. But have an organized group come in from outside and get on ladders and start climbing around trees on your property, that would have potentially given people pause," Lee says. "So what we figured out was the waivers and all that . . . once you could assure people this is all legit and there's no risk in it, or you could take some of the risk out, that started to allay people's concerns."

The third element was a formula — that one quarter of the harvest would go to the homeowner, one quarter to the volunteer pickers, one quarter to a community agency and one quarter to the organization. The numbers play out differently in various areas now, "but the idea that there was a formula and that part of the benefit of the fruit wasn't just going to a bunch of hippies who showed up on your doorstep but rather to support the truly poor in the city, I think also made the program more accessible to people. It got them past the 'what's in it for me?' piece."

Lee and Matt are both hazy on the details of their first pick. Matt is sure the work team picked apples that went to young mothers in need. Lee thinks they may have gone to Mustard Seed, a local food bank.

They were a good match. Both had a strong social conscience, an interest in the environment and food and an entrepreneurial bent. Both were fans of Elliot Coleman, an American organic farmer and writer who served with the International Federation of Organic Agriculture Movements. Matt had been involved with what was then an emerging movement of antiglobal protests at the 1997 APEC Summit in Vancouver. The protests were marked by clashes with police involving pepper spray, dogs and multiple arrests. "I realized I wasn't really an activist in the purest sense," he says. "I was more interested in the building aspects and translating that activism into real life, on-the-ground attempts to create new systems and new ways to do things."

Even today, almost 20 years later, Matt and Lee think alike: both use the term "anarchists" to describe the ideologically minded, and both still hope for a business model that can help sustain good works with less, if any, reliance on grants and donations.

Into the second year, Lee and Matt went back to LifeCycles with their project handily proven. The organization agreed to take it on. Lee had started a paid job working at BC Stats, the provincial statistical agency. His office was across the street from LifeCycles, so he'd pop over for lunch to help mentor the coordinators. He stayed involved for a while, happy to have handed the project off and to see it grow. Matt headed to Brazil to work with the International Council for Local Environmental Initiatives. He lives in Vancouver now.

As back-to-the-land as these outfits all seem, none of them works without funding. You'd have to be very devoted with endless time to spare to run a program of this kind as a volunteer. Even then, you'd need the equivalent of Lee's $100 infusion to get even the most basic organization running. That only gets a corkboard and coloured pins, so harvesting organizations turn to grants and donations and join the list of worthy causes in the charitable sector competing for the largess of others. Winnipeg's Fruit Share and Edmonton's Operation Fruit Rescue charge membership fees that allow cardholders to participate in picks, register trees and take part in workshops on using fruit.

The idea of making the harvest organization self-sustaining is what Lee envisioned. In that early pamphlet, he says, "If this pilot proves successful, the future for the project is wide open . . . A wide variety of products can be made from these fruits — securing a high-quality local supply could provide opportunities for all sorts of micro-businesses as an offshoot of the project: juicing, saucing, making pies, drying, jam, jellies . . ."

Sustainability was a hot topic through the '80s and '90s, and Lee had his own take on it. "I didn't just see that as environmental sustainability. What that meant to me was that everything had to be more or less on a paying basis." That's the challenge for many community organizations, he says. "They don't think about the long-term sustainability of the project and so they get funding driven and funding dependent." Fernwood, where he works now, is known across the city as being entrepreneurial and involved in social enterprise. "From the beginning, I saw the potential of this as basically an urban orchard in the same way that you've got people now who make deals and farm in the city in people's backyards." It's called SPIN farming, an acronym for "small plot intensive." Sub-acre plots are rented or bartered in exchange for produce. The idea is to help new farmers get into the business without having to buy land. "They are selling very high-end quality produce to people who are picky, and restaurants. And they can do a good trade."

I tell him about what's going on in Ottawa, where one of the newer harvest organizations has blossomed. Rather than a manifesto, Hidden Harvest started with a business model with specific year-by-year goals. It aims for a blended return on investment that is financial, social and environmental. The social and environmental parts are easy to quantify — using existing produce and sharing it with people in need. But the financial part has no guarantee. In addition to picking, Hidden Harvest has experimented with selling trees and jams and looked at making juices to support the enterprise. Cofounder Katrina Siks says it's been a roller coaster searching for the piece that works without costing staff time. "We're really careful about not incurring overhead costs. We have no phone, no office and no storage," Siks says. Equipment is stored in volunteers' basements. Although it has corporate sponsors that share profits for volunteer labour and promotional considerations, the organization runs without relying on grants.

"Perfect," Lee says.

Hidden Harvest's ultimate goal is to foster the largest urban orchard in Eastern Canada. That's a pretty bold statement but in line with Lee's thinking for an urban harvester. Here's what he wrote in the original pamphlet: "The fruit trees in Victoria represent a local inheritance from our forebears who planted the trees in the first place. Who shall plant trees for our grandchildren if we won't?"

The brochure included talk about harvesting rare scions — spurs from buds — to graft and ensure the continuity of the trees. Perhaps the larger gift was creating the Fruit Tree Project. There are more than a dozen organizations across the country and many more in the U.S. using Lee and Matt's model to collect unwanted fruit. "The fact that it's still around is the thing that makes me the most happy," says Matt. "It's one of the things I've done that I'm most proud of."

Lee says the model's fecundity is fantastic. He had pushed people in the early years to say, "This is a movement we're starting. So let's share information." I ask about a franchising model. It might have generated income too. "There were thoughts about how can we benefit from that, and I said it doesn't matter. We just want people to be doing this everywhere." He's keen on selling products, but not ideas. It's an interesting approach in the information age.

As the Victoria Fruit Tree Project carried on under LifeCycles' banner, Lee stayed in touch but developed new interests. He doesn't pick fruit anymore, and he lives in a basement suite with a small south-facing window with not enough light for even herbs. Still, he doesn't let himself off the hook, "'Cause that will just be a too-tragic ending to my story."

The tiny orchard by the skateboarders keeps his toe in the fruit game. Volunteers planted 25 trees in 2013 as an investment in the neighbourhood's future. And it's another step toward one of the early goals of the Fruit Tree Project. In that first brochure, Lee quoted architect and author Christopher Alexander:

> *Fruit trees on common land add much more to the neighbourhood and the community than the same trees in private backyards: privately grown, the trees tend to produce more fruit than one household can consume. On public land, the trees concentrate the feeling of mutual benefit and responsibility. And because they require yearly care, pruning, and harvesting, the fruit trees naturally involve people in their common land. . . . Imagine a community gradually being able to produce a portion of its own need for fruit, or cider, or preserves . . .*

Lee is thinking about his contribution to the city fruit world. He combined his practical knowledge of what it means to pick fruit from the farm with "a theoretical idea of breaking down the problem of fruit trees on private land, where they exceed the capacity of the homeowners to manage it. It's more of a burden than a benefit." But he cautions me against giving "undue credit to the guy with the idea," more than that due to the people who spend afternoons picking fruit. "I saw my contribution as being more the task of thinking it through and making it work, which obviously seems to have been a useful thing to have done. "You know, the idea of picking your neighbour's tree and sharing it with them is no big deal."

It may be no big deal on the individual level, but cumulatively, the thousands of hands shaking hands under fruit trees has turned out to be a spectacular benefit for communities far beyond Victoria.

QUINCE PASTE
(GLUTEN-FREE, VEGAN)

Quince paste is consumed in many parts of the world and may have been the base for the first marmalades. In Portuguese, quince is called "*marmelo,*" and the jam from it "*marmelada.*" When I asked new friends from Syria what fruit they most missed from their home country, they named quince.

LifeCycles Fruit Tree Project in Victoria sells this quince paste to help keep the project running.

This recipe from LifeCycles can be made in small batches following the proportions indicated.

INGREDIENTS

Entire quince fruits
Sugar

* For baking quince paste, use stainless steel 4-sided pans that are not too thick — the big rectangle ones (13 x 9) worked well but the smaller ones that have an extra thick bottom did not work. Smaller pans with normal thickness bottoms also work well.

INSTRUCTIONS

1. *Preheat oven to 375°F.*
2. *Prepare quince by removing bad spots, although*

uncut quince is ideal. Lay whole quince (including cores) on baking trays 1 layer deep.

3. Bake in oven for approximately 45 minutes until skin is brownish and/or starting to come away from the fruit. Remove quince from oven and cool.

4. Once cool enough to handle, peel and core quince with knife and/or hands. (This process works much better if the fruit is completely cooled.) Discard skin and cores. Place quince pulp in containers.

5. Weigh pulp and record then transfer into a large steam kettle. Add half sugar by weight (i.e., for every 1 lb of quince pulp, add ½ lb sugar).

6. Stir over low heat until thick and quince pieces are soft and sugar has dissolved and caramelized (approximately 3 hours). Puree with blender.

7. Prepare baking pans by lightly spraying with veggie nonstick spray and line with parchment.

8. Turn off steam kettle once paste is smooth and dark and gelling (test by putting in the fridge for a short period). Pour paste 1½ inches deep onto pans.

9. Place pans in very low heat oven (approximately 75 degrees) with fan on high (if you have a fanned oven). Leave pans in oven

*overnight or for about 10 hours. Label oven so
no one opens it.*

10. *In the morning, remove and put quince paste
    on cooling racks, then repeat with same time
    and temperature for a second night. (You could
    probably do this step all at once, i.e., 15 hours
    straight with no break.)*

11. *When cool, cut into desired shapes, wrap in
    plastic and refrigerate. (In the 17th century,
    quince pastes were often decorated using wooden
    moulds.)*

CHAPTER THREE

UP A TREE

THE EXPERIENCE

A lyrical dee-dum signals a new email. It's from Not Far From The Tree announcing another fruit pick. There can't be many left. Apples this time, and the location looks close. I head to the portal to the click-through process.

I've signed up as a volunteer to get a first-hand look at all the ignored fruit in the city. It seems like a simple thing to do. Volunteer to pick someone's unwanted fruit and cart it away for them. But I've moved fast on several notices only to find that, within minutes, I'm ninth on the waiting list. A veteran told me she leaves the web page open when her favourite fruits are in season, refreshing every few minutes to catch the new listings first.

Someone else's discards have become treasures to this band of fruit hunters. Supply and demand usually drive up prices — I think of the ubiquitous coloured Pyrex bowls of the '50s, now a coveted find in vintage stores. But in this case, we're after free, locally grown, probably pesticide-free fruit. There are plenty of heritage trees in the city and plenty of people who want to pick them. The stumbling block is the infrastructure and costs required to connect the two. I'm curious to see who these people are and whether it's really the fruit they are after.

I feel like a young intern, competing for the experience of working for free. Of course, this won't define my career, but I'm caught up in the chase and now I want to win.

The emails are always friendly. Still, when you've seen four of them in one day without success, the cheeriness gets a bit irksome. There are details about what to wear and how to cancel and then the closing, "Fruitfully Yours, Not Far From The Tree."

Dundas and High Park is close enough. I could walk there. Sour apples. Would I use them? Throw in some sugar and make a sauce? There's no time to consider the details. I click "accept." I'm on the wait list. Darn. By the end of the day, my luck turns. I'm in.

The day of the pick arrives with gloomy skies and sweatshirt weather. The apple tree is just blocks away on my own street. I pedal up the road midafternoon past my old high school. The back field is empty today, grass scuffed from field hockey sticks and football cleats. As I ride past, I can picture heading onto the field again. But who am I kidding? I had let my fitness slide through the summer as I recovered from pneumonia. I can feel the results in my lungs and legs, even on this short trip uphill.

A minute later, I pull into the driveway of the secret address. A sugar maple shadows the third-floor windows, and pots of flowering plants line the stone steps to the porch. Over the past few decades I've done a lot of political canvassing and always enjoy doing "drops," stuffing pamphlets or other campaign literature into mailboxes. You seldom meet anyone, so you can relax your persuasion skills and slip into a monk-like mindfulness. Pull the card from the bundle, lift the lid of the mailbox, drop, close and move on. You also get a lot of exercise moving from house to house, climbing stairs and searching for mailboxes. I try to imagine personality types from the clues left outside. Are the yards wild and natural or manicured and minimalist? Is the porch furniture carefully curated or is the space a jumble of children's scooters and bikes? Does the aroma of bacon and coffee drift through the screen midmorning or are onions and garlic stewing for later?

Fruit picking brings me past the front door to the private sanctuary of the backyard. Before I started my quest, I spoke to Juby Lee, the project coordinator of Environment Hamilton's Fruit Tree Project. Juby has been picking for years, harvesting fruit in the port city at the tip of Lake Ontario. Hamilton is well known for its steel industry, but it also has a lot of fruit. It's on the edge of the soft fruit belt of Ontario and has a substantial Italian population — people who brought to Canada a tradition of homegrown produce. Part of Juby's job is finding homeowners willing to open their back gates. She has a great appreciation for their generosity. "In this time of liability, when people could say 'stay off my property,' it's a very sweet relationship," she told me. "Here is a private space that you would never have access to and here's a moment when the homeowner says 'come on in.'"

As I wheel up to the address, Alison Smith opens the front door and I introduce myself. Although she and I live on the same street, we're too many blocks apart to have connected. But she does exactly what Juby celebrated. "Come on in," she says.

I head up the asphalt driveway, carefully pushing my bike past a parked car and toe down the kickstand in front of the garage. Alison meets me by the back door, buttoning her pea coat as she steps out.

Shielded by greenery from city noise and concrete, the yard must be an oasis after a long day at work. Alison works in communications for the provincial government and with her husband has teenaged children. We have a lot in common, so it's not hard to imagine a Friday night barbecue on the flagstone patio, sitting under the vine-covered pergola. Perhaps the kids when younger would have played tag or run through a sprinkler on the lawn that spreads out behind the garage, mature trees shading them from the late-day sun.

We sit together on an iron bench and I explain my project, how we've lost the knowledge about what to do with fruit trees.

"I fit right into that category," Alison shrugs. "I don't know how to identify them."

Her apple tree reaches the eavestrough. It is laden with fruit, plenty of it half-eaten by raccoons and squirrels. Even the creatures create waste. I wonder what stops them from finishing or coming back to the same piece. "Honestly I'm not sure our apples are OK," Alison says when I mention this, adding that years ago she picked some for a pie but the experience left her wanting. "They're tiny, so it's really hard to cut them up and core them. They're super hard and super sour, so I had to add a lot of sugar. The pie was decent, but it seemed like three times more work than just buying apples from the grocery store."

The apples on the ground don't match the oversized fruits we picked at the one-hundred-acre pick-your-own apple farm the weekend previous or most of the fruit I find in grocery stores. These ones are freckled with brown spots and the surfaces are uneven. "There's not a lot of meat from these guys," Alison says, flipping a hand at the animals' leftovers, "so that was my one pie."

But she remembers it.

Toward the end of *The Omnivore's Dilemma*, Michael Pollan prepares a dinner from food made entirely from meat, vegetables and fruit he has harvested himself. He knows it's not practical for every day but, he writes, "no meal I've ever prepared or eaten has been more real."

Being able to say "I made it myself" has always appealed to me. I'm an easy touch at bake sales, especially when the chef is counting the sticky change and can tell me exactly what's in the butter tarts. Pollan sums that up nicely in his prologue. "The pleasures of eating . . . are only deepened by knowing."

That pie Alison made would have been all the more pleasurable, knowing the work it took to produce it. Alison didn't plant the tree. It was here when she and her husband bought the house in the late '90s from a couple who must have loved gardening. Flower beds, fruit trees and interesting shapes to the landscaping would have taken years of work to create. But, judging by the tree's height and Alison's recollection of that couple's age, they wouldn't have planted it either. So three families have watched it grow, I say, asking her what was here when they moved in. "The apple tree was here; there was a cherry tree in front of the shed." She hesitates, drawing a breath and bracing for my reaction to her next comment: "which we cut down." She looks away then tries a recovery. "It wasn't doing very well, it was dying, I think, so . . ." She deflates with a big breath out. "Feeding right into your thesis."

I nod in understanding and look as if to see what's no longer there.

Alison points to a second cherry tree at the back of the property that's doing fine. It's well past the roof lines and, without the fruit on it now, I wouldn't have guessed it to be a cherry. "We don't really pick those cherries either," she confesses. "It's a feast for the raccoons." And the neighbour, she tells me, complains bitterly about the mess in her yard.

Alison looks almost guilty. I offer a sympathetic smile. I am trying to keep an open mind. Who isn't busy? We've calibrated our modern world with a lot of distractions and obligations.

We shift on the bench; I push a half-eaten apple from under my feet and Alison sweeps a leaf aside. Maybe we all feel guilty about wasting food or knowing more about wine pairings than how to grow and use a grape.

Alison turns to the grapevines climbing the sides of a brown-stained pergola. The vines are two thumbs thick. They must have been here for decades. But there is no fruit to be seen. Grapes can live and keep on producing for a long time, so I'm curious. Enter the raccoons again, Alison explains. The grapes were so delectable to the mask-wearing beasts that the ground was littered with scat every morning, a big city concern, particularly in yards where young children play. The grapes had to go. They've been replaced by wisteria. I look closer and see the stumps six feet up, the floral vines winding around them.

As she tours me through the garden, Alison tells me she grew up in Montreal with a green-thumbed mom and a yard with a crabapple tree and raspberry bushes. Then she points out another plant: "Oh, we have this guy. This guy has some fruit, some sort of a berry."

It's probably a weeping mulberry, I tell her.

"Yeah, maybe," she nods. "We eat those because it's very convenient. You can just pick them off and eat them."

Maybe? I'm a bit baffled. "So you eat them but you don't know what they are?"

"I think someone identified them," she backtracks, looking down. "My mom came . . . "

Food Secure Canada, Ontario's Home Economists and Harvard University are among the many organizations lobbying for programs to improve food literacy. A Conference Board of Canada report on improving food literacy called *What's to Eat?* incorporates an understanding of how food is processed as part of that literacy. Each organization talks about the wider issue of knowing what's good for you. I've spoken to many offspring of immigrants who admit they don't know half of what was planted in their grandparents' yards or how to use it. It is a collective loss. "It's too bad," Alison says.

Val Colden strides into the yard. She is also a volunteer and trained to lead harvests, a "Supreme Gleaner," as Not Far From The Tree puts it. The supremes run the picks, make sure everyone is safe and carry the equipment in and the fruit out. They also compete for opportunities. I am introduced to quite a few supremes during my tours, and Val is particularly thorough. She's also been with the organization since its inception.

After explaining the drill to Alison, Val heaves equipment into the yard: pick poles, canvas bags, a hand-held weigh scale, paper yard waste bags and white plastic buckets with body harnesses — so pickers can keep both hands free. I recognize Val's lettuce-green T-shirt embossed with a taupe sketch of trees making a canopy for a distant city. It's an original from NFFTT, already vintage for a seven-year-old organization. Val pulls it over her hips, unsnaps her bike helmet and gets the equipment ready. Two more women slip into the yard. Debi Brennen and Heather O'Shea say their hellos, drop their bags on the table and take a look at the tree. Val starts filling us in on the instructions. The pre-pick speech is mandatory. Clean up the windfall first, never use a ladder without someone spotting, don't do more than you can, keep the fallen fruit separate. You can take it home if you want, but we can't donate it.

I remember the raccoon scat and think I might give it a pass too.

"And finally," Val says, "beware of fruit greed. We all know that the best fruits are the pieces just out of reach, at the top of the tree where there is more sun." She tells us to go no higher than the second-last rung of the ladder. Don't take risks for what may seem like the pick of the crop. Pratfalls from the top rung are only funny in the movies. Falling off a ladder can end with years of treatment. A lot of pickers won't climb. I like being up high in the tree. It brings me to another world, one with a different perspective.

Tree Climbers International touts the benefits of being up a tree, including exercise, accessibility and a full sensory experience with hands on bark and the sound of wind whistling through leaves. Japan is home to a tree-climbing school and has led the way in using trees for a lot of therapy. Through a Tree Climbing Japan program called TreeHab, a 57-year-old woman left her wheelchair in 2001 and became the first paraplegic person in the world to climb 78 metres up a Sequoia tree. Researchers have started looking at the growing popularity of climbing on branches. A group at Japan's Nagoya University found marked differences in outcomes between climbing a concrete tower with an artificial branch and climbing a real tree. John Gathright, Yozo Yamada and Miyako Morita concluded, "Climbers' bodies were more relaxed after tree climbing than after tower climbing. Psychological results indicated greater vitality, and reduced tension, confusion, and fatigue while tree climbing, when compared to tower climbing."

Japan has developed a body of expertise in trees as therapy. In 1982, Japan's Forest Agency, a government body, introduced the concept of *shinrin-yoku*, which translates roughly into "forest bathing." The idea is to spend time among trees as an aid to physical and mental health. Forty minutes of walking is the ideal. Researchers found that not only did the forest walkers feel better, they showed lower levels of the stress hormone cortisol than test subjects who walked in a laboratory. Eva Selhub and Alan Logan sum up the research in their book *Your Brain on Nature*. The practice is more commonly known now as forest medicine. The International Society of Nature and Forest Medicine (INFOM) advances the concept and collects scientific data on human stress reduction from spending time with trees. It's also putting forward research that shows that forest bathing can activate human natural killer cells, a part of the immune system that works against cancer.

Alison offers us gardening gloves. For a nongardener she has a lot of pairs, although I note they look brand new. "They were on sale," she laughs, handing them out before grabbing a rake and heading to the golden-yellow leaves scattered on the grass.

Preliminary cleanup complete, we each grab a pole

to start on the tree. If you want to see a natural apple tree today, head to a city. This one is virtually growing wild. It's unsprayed, unpruned and unpicked but for the animals' efforts. As we start reaching and climbing, I think of the orchards we've visited where even the youngest kids can fill a bag without so much as a step stool. Many of the trees are trained and pruned like vines, supported by a horizontal line of wiring. Espalier pruning, as it's called, still seems odd to see in North America, where our image of an apple tree is something you can sit under. The espaliered trees look more like two-dimensional candelabras. The term comes from the Italian word *"spalliera,"* referring to a support for a shoulder or back.

Although some believe a similar process was carried out by the Romans, the practice has been around formally since the 16th century. Farmers in colder parts of France and England used it to create a microclimate for growing fruit along warm walls, protected on one side from the elements. I was surprised to learn that, just like today, it was also used to grow fruit in small spaces. Writing for the *Arnoldia*, the magazine of Harvard University's Arnold Arboretum, horticulturalist Lee Reich answers the question of why anyone would go to all the trouble of snipping, pruning and tying branches relentlessly. "Because a well-grown espalier represents a happy commingling of art and science, resulting in a plant that pleases not only the eye, but also the palate."

Not all farmers are worried about the eye candy.

Many are moving to "size-controlled" or dwarf trees to increase efficiency. Ontario's Ministry of Agriculture describes the trend toward "pedestrian orchards where practices can be carried out with minimum use of ladders." In other words, you can pick a lot faster, and probably longer, if you aren't climbing.

Here in Alison's backyard, we extend our aluminum poles to their full 10 feet. Two of us start on the deck and soon add a ladder to the mix. I hold the ladder, spotting for Heather, who is skilled with the pole. I find out later she too is a supreme gleaner. She's also a sign language translator and a swing dance instructor, and she recently did a stint at a farm workshare, trading labour for vegetables. I watch her technique. Lift, twist, wait for the drop. The pick poles are lightweight, topped with claws fanging inward at the mouth of bright blue-and-yellow canvas bags. Two hours slip by quickly, but I can imagine the muscle tone professional pickers must have. "My arms start to ache after three apples," Heather says, lowering the bag so I can empty it.

We switch places and I get in a tug-of-war with an apple just beyond the pole's reach. Through the leaves, sunlight strobes off the skin, taunting me. I pull hard, the apple flies past the claw and then there's the thud of fruit hitting something hard. I look down to see Heather rubbing the crown of her head. "I'm sorry!" the words fly out of my mouth. "That's OK," she answers, still rubbing her curls. I'm glad it missed the sunglasses perched above her forehead. "I probably should have been hit by now. This is the first time. That was a good one too; it was nice and heavy." She lets out a hearty laugh.

All of the apples are spotted. Still, Val eats one and pronounces it good. I look for an unmarked piece and bite in. The flavour is sweet but the texture a bit mealy. Perhaps Alison picked too soon and we are picking too late. I compare my one-big-bite teeth marks to the scratchy etchings left by the squirrels. Heather goes back up the ladder. She tells me she travelled an hour and a half on public transit to get here. Living in Scarborough, at the eastern edge of the city, she says it's a 90-minute trip anywhere, so she doesn't worry about that. But she really wanted the apples. I think she must be disappointed in the quality, but I'm wrong. It doesn't matter when you are making cider.

"I've been holding on to batches all summer. They're just waiting until I have enough volume." She needs 20 pounds of apples to make a gallon, but she was yielding just one or two on each pick in August. She insists it's worth the wait and patience. "From each pick you're getting a different variety, so it's a more complex-flavour cider."

I'm picturing the payoff in months of cider lined up on shelves to get through the winter. Heather sets me straight: "If I'm sharing, it might only last a night."

Wow. I'm doing the math on hours spent versus time consumed, but it's a pointless exercise. We are all enjoying ourselves. Val and Debi are deep into a discussion about knitting socks, where to get the best hand-dyed yarns and the perils of second-sock syndrome. Apparently it's a thing. Socks are just the tip of Debi's crafting. She upcycles paper products, mostly magazines and comic books, into belts, wallets, messenger bags and corsets. I will have to go to her Etsy site and see for myself. She's also a writer and cosplay blogger, capturing in words the adventures of people who dress up like fictional — often anime or sci-fi — characters. Think Spock ears as a starting point.

While we've picked, Alison has quietly raked the yard, gently pulling the leaves toward her. She slips back into the house, she tells us, to kickstart the homework.

We keep picking and Heather asks about my research. She's wondering if Hamilton has a similar program. She's thinking of moving there for the lower-cost real estate, but she'd really miss Not Far From The Tree. I tell her about Juby Lee and the Fruit Tree Project. It started years before Toronto's harvest group. "That makes me want to move there more." She smiles. I'm imagining her bolstering another plank in her campaign to convince a reluctant boyfriend that Steeltown is a progressive place. Debi, it turns out, once lived in Hamilton, so the sourcing continues.

We're nearing the end of finding reachable fruit. Debi and Val are cleaning up the patio, Heather and I are alternating on the ladder. The crack of an apple hitting the flagstone followed by a quick "Eiieeh! Whoooah!" from below breaks the conversation. "That was impressive," Val says. The apple just missed her.

I'm struggling with another fruit. It doesn't surrender

until the pole jerks up and the branch is empty. I've got it. Val cheers me on. "We'll show you, apple!"

As we tidy up and get ready for the weigh-in, the talk turns to food. Heather is a forager. She picks dandelions, garlic mustard and sumac from wild spaces in the city. She's also filled her kitchen with five different varieties of jam. Debi made peach salsa this summer, which opened a discussion on where to find the best peaches. That led us to Dave Masumoto, an organic farmer in California who has made a side career writing about his efforts to save what he insists is the perfect peach, the Sun Crest. His seven books on farming and food started with a 1987 article in the *Los Angeles Times* about deciding whether to bulldoze the no-longer-popular variety. No one was buying them, but the article prompted an outpouring of support from readers urging him to spare the trees. I think of the protests against logging in areas many of us will never visit. I know it's more complicated than that, but a politician once called these places "the greenspace of the mind." I think there is something to that, something that comforts us. Knowing such places exist. Just in case.

Maybe it's a romantic notion of farm life or saving peaches. Masumoto did save those peaches, but in his first book, *Epitaph for a Peach*, he writes of losing a season of near-ready sun-dried raisins to rain. Not much romance in that.

But Debi is certain the best peaches are in Winona, Ontario, her hometown. Heather agrees. "Last year we went to Niagara and I had the best peaches ever. They were sweet and juicy and amazing."

On every pick, I hear a lot about jams and a lot of discussion about food security. I float the idea that the two aren't connected. That as much as we might like it, we don't really *need* jam.

"No," Heather agrees, "although you could live off it."

Barely. While it might keep you alive if you were lost in the woods, our bodies need more than fruit to flourish. Writing for the Mayo Clinic, registered dietitians Jennifer Nelson and Katherine Zeratsky say fruit and vegetables are nutritionally similar. Both "contain health-enhancing plant compounds such as antioxidants. And they're loaded with vitamins and minerals." Ignoring potatoes, vegetables tend to have fewer calories than fruit. If you're watching your sugar intake, the sugar content is higher in fruit (although it's natural) even without turning it into jam. A chart compiled by the Canadian Produce Marketing Association shows that an apple, for example, contains 15 grams of sugar while a half stalk of broccoli contains one gram. The broccoli is a far better source of vitamin C.

But no single food, whether fruit or vegetable, can give us all the nutrition we need. That said, in the U.S. between 1999 and 2008, servings of fruit and vegetables declined by about 10 percent and 7 percent, respectively. So in that country, any increase in intake would be a good thing. Like for the early explorers, not getting enough of the stuff that comes from the ground, trees and bushes has consequences. Eating fruits and vegetables plays a role in preventing cancer, heart disease, high blood pressure, stroke and diabetes.

Heather admits that not all of the foraging food, which may be good for you, tastes good. Dandelion roots, for example, are a little bitter, she says, "but if you dry them out and grind them, they make a drink like coffee which is cool."

That's a lot of work, again, for something we don't need. But Heather likes what it stands for. "It's nice to know if ever there was a day when there was some kind of embargo or no way to get coffee from the countries that produce them, I could still get a coffee-like drink by myself."

Val calls it a day and ends the pick. She figures we've got all we can, and she has to get the fruit to a neighbourhood food bank before it closes. It's one of the many details that make this simple act of picking city fruit more involved than it seems. Alison rejoins us as we bag up the apples. Heather holds the scale, hanging each bag by the straps. Val directs the distribution and recording.

Green bag: 15 ½ pounds
Black President's Choice bag: 23 pounds
Walmart Halloween bag: 19 pounds
Windfall in a white bag: 14 ½ pounds

The only one carrying pen and paper, I make the quick calculation. Seventy-two pounds of fruit off one untended tree. Alison declines her share, so two-thirds will go to charity and one third to the pickers. We'll each get six pounds to take home, roughly a $12 payment for two hours of work, but we're not here for the cost benefit. "Awesome! Nice!" We're feeling good. Alison gives us a big smile. "That's amazing."

What's becoming more amazing to me is that we've captured just one tree in a city with a million like it. Picking the fruit was a simple thing for Debi and Heather and me, but we wouldn't have been here without the network of the organization. So Lee is right that the idea is simple. It's connecting the pickers to the trees that gets complicated, and now we have to move the fruit.

We rebag the apples into shares for each of us and leave the yard. I turn back for one more look. The tree looks lighter but a little sadder without its fruit. It's the Christmas tree on January 2, standing in the corner without its bling.

Val waits for me at the end of the driveway with the keys to the cargo bike dangling from a finger. I had asked the administrators if I could do a ride-along, but I wasn't expecting to be the driver.

Not Far From The Tree limits its carbon footprint by using only bikes to transport harvests. That restricts where the organization can pick, but speaks to its focus on environmental sustainability. Founder Laura Reinsborough has told me the model works in Toronto because there are typically just one or two trees on each property. The cargo bikes can carry up to 220 pounds, "a perfect solution for that scale."

Today's harvest is going to the Sharing Place, a food bank and source of community meals. I've passed it many times. I don't think it's too far, but I'm looking at the bike, now loaded with one hundred pounds of fruit and equipment, and mentally mapping the route, hoping there aren't any hills. I haven't done much biking this summer, or anything else physical for that matter. I've meant to get my fitness levels back up but . . . I take a breath and steel myself. This is where the excuses stop.

Val has brought two bags of grapes she picked the day before in the next riding east. She's jerry-rigged two square plastic tubs with metal hooks to hang from the sides of the rear rack as panniers. As if we need to add more weight.

As a kid, I could hang a jug of milk from the handlebars or ride with no hands without any trouble. But with a bucket attached to the front it's a challenge to balance and steer. In an earlier joyride the organization offered at a city festival, I hit a parked car. I'm glad today's ride is a three-wheeler, much easier to manoeuvre. The leather seat is in front of the single back wheel, and the apple-embossed red cargo hold is held up on either side by two front wheels.

Val reminds me to take my time — no worries there

— and to leave room for wide turns. I climb on and put my feet on the pedals. It moves. I brake. It stops. Good. I start again and my first turn out of the driveway lands me in the middle of the road. I'm thankful it's Sunday and nearing the supper hour. The streets are quiet and there's no one watching. I start to pedal. I'm doing it, although I'm feeling small, like I've borrowed my big sister's bike. Val is up ahead on my bike, gliding effortlessly. She's trying to match my pace, but I'm going so slow she's a bit wobbly. We make it past 24 addresses to the corner and I signal to turn right. It's a much busier street but, mercifully, there is a bike lane. Just a strip of white paint on the asphalt, but I will command the space. A bus pulls past, giving me a wide berth. Smart driver. I was picturing myself sprawled on the sidewalk with an upset apple cart — a metaphor come to life. At a dip in the road, I can pedal harder, but that feeling that I've got this is fading. It seems my street is on enough of a slope to have made the first stretch easy. And now we're sloping upward. Oh dear.

I flip the gears, trying to make the ride easier. I'm embarrassed by how low I've dialled on a stretch that no one would call a hill. My quads burn and I stop talking to Val. People on the sidewalk are watching. I can't look at them. We pass two schools, a coffee shop, butcher and convenience store. We're through a big intersection and then I see the beacon ahead. The blue-and-white sign pokes out from the buildings on the next block.

The Sharing Place is run by Grace Church of the

Nazarene in a tidy red-brick building with a simple white spire matching the main door trim. But I don't see any of it as I pedal into the parking lot. Now my whole body has had enough. I feel the weakness that comes from too little food and too much exercise. Only this time, it may be the opposite.

Val flips the grape bins off the bike and barrels toward the door, arms loaded with fruit. I stare at the 40 pounds of apples I'll have to carry. I keep on faking that everything's fine, really wishing I could just sit down for a minute.

A group of teenagers chat in Spanish, clustered at the front door. One holds it open for us as we hurry up the steps. The church runs two services, one in English in the morning and another in Spanish in the afternoon. They've just finished and we've made it before the doors lock at six.

A thin dark-haired man directs us down the stairs to a large dining room, round tables empty now after what was probably a time of postworship fellowship. He seems to have no interest in the delivery. A few women sit at a scattering of tables chatting. Another woman comes from a back door to the kitchen counter at the side and starts transferring the grapes to large bowls. "They look good," she says before she notices they are leaking juice everywhere. She clicks her tongue, annoyed. I see another large container of yellow apples on the floor. No spots and bigger than ours. I'm having apple envy.

I ask the woman trying to mop up the mess with paper towel what they'll do with the fruit. She doesn't know.

"Pastor Gena is in charge." Our two hours of picking seems inadequate.

A young boy rushes in and tells "Sister" that Pastor Gena is ready. Sister takes us up to wait. Gena Torres is in the sanctuary slipping on a pink coat. She hurries to catch us, purse and bags on her arm. She extends her warm hand and thanks us both. She may be "in charge," but her presence is more generous than commanding. A blond bob frames a soft, round face. Rectangular tortoiseshell glasses sit above full cheeks. She tells us the fruit is always welcome and means a lot to the clients of the Sharing Place. I tell her it appears we've caught her at a busy time and can I . . . "Yes, I'm on my way," she finishes for me. "I have to see my son in hospital." But she agrees to speak tomorrow. "Anytime," she says, and I think she means it. I take her cellphone number.

As we resettle on the bikes, Gena walks toward her car but stops to admire the cargo rig. Val proudly explains the transport process: "You've got apples and grapes that have never been in a motorized vehicle or a fridge. They're hyper-local."

Gena thanks us again.

We're off. This time, Val is on the cargo bike and I'm back to my own wheels. We head a few blocks north and into a laneway, rolling the bike into donated garage space, valuable real estate in Toronto.

A few weeks later, I check in to see what Val's done with her apples. She's pressed them into juice and turned it into cider. "It's still sitting on the top of my fridge," she writes. "I have to get it bottled soon."

Most of my share went into shredded cabbage with cider vinegar, a dish that took minutes to prepare (hours of apple picking aside). But the prep time didn't really matter. Having seen where the apples grew and realizing that they came not just from the work of my own hands, but from the people who lived on this street long before me, gave them, as Michael Pollan observed about food he had harvested himself, a distinct flavour of knowing.

CHOCOLATE PEAR TART IN A CHOCOLATE ALMOND CRUST (GLUTEN-FREE)

Manitoba Fruit Share founder Getty Stewart created this recipe, which she made with pears picked by volunteers in Winnipeg and with BC Bartlett pears. The combination of smooth dark chocolate custard, ground almonds and pears makes it one of her favourite recipes.

The original version was published in *The Prairie Fruit Cookbook* by Getty Stewart.

Yields one 9- to 10-inch tart.

INGREDIENTS

CRUST

1½ cups finely ground almonds

3 tbsp sugar

1 oz semisweet chocolate

⅓ cup butter

FILLING

2 oz semisweet chocolate

½ cup whipping cream

2 tbsp sugar

2 eggs, separated

1 tsp almond extract

2 pears, fresh or canned

INSTRUCTIONS

CHOCOLATE ALMOND CRUST

1. Mix almonds and sugar in a medium bowl.
2. Melt chocolate in a separate bowl.
3. Melt butter and mix into chocolate.
4. Mix chocolate and butter into the almond mix and stir until well blended.
5. Pour into a 9- or 10-inch (23- to 25-cm) tart pan or springform pan.
6. Press mixture evenly into pan and ½ inch (1.2 cm) up the sides.
7. Refrigerate until needed.

FILLING

1. In a medium pot on medium heat, melt chocolate in cream, stirring constantly.
2. Remove pot from heat and cool.
3. Mix sugar, egg yolks and almond extract. Add to chocolate mix.
4. Heat slowly on medium heat, stirring constantly. Do not boil.
5. Heat for 3 minutes until mixture is smooth and thick.
6. Beat egg whites until stiff peaks form.
7. Mix ⅓ of egg whites into chocolate mixture.
8. Gently fold in remaining egg whites.

ASSEMBLY

1. *Preheat oven to 350 °F (180 °C).*
2. *Pour the batter into the crust and place pears on top in your preferred pear design (half pears, sliced pears, arranged in circles, flower shape, diagonals, clusters, etc.).*
3. *Bake in centre of oven for 30 minutes or until chocolate mixture has set.*
4. *Remove from oven and cool before slicing.*

CHAPTER FOUR

THE FRUITS OF
OUR LABOUR

SHARING THE BOUNTY

I head back to the Sharing Place a few days later. Even from the parking lot, it's evident this is no Sunday-only church. A bit tight for time on this Tuesday morning, I've left my bike at home and am driving the minivan. There are spots open, but not many.

A screwdriver holds the side door slightly ajar. A waft of warm air with the church-basement smell of daycare hits my nose — laundry, bleach, hand-me-downs and an undertone of diapers. Voices and kids' laughter lead me to the donated clothing area, a dimly lit, windowless room downstairs. It could be a small second-hand shop, garments neatly hung and shoes lined up in pairs. A man and two women flipping through the racks look up at my arrival.

"I'm here to see Pastor Gena," I say, hoping I haven't interrupted something private. They could be volunteers or clients, and I'm mindful of respecting privacy, especially since I'm in my own neighbourhood. "Through there," one points to the right. The door leads to an anteroom of tables and boxes, then into the dining room and kitchen. The tables are empty this morning, but the place is buzzing with activity. T-shirted tweens are squealing at something and rushing through the rooms. "Guys," warns a petite grey-haired woman. She's working at a counter piled high with bags of breads and rolls. The kids move on, finding a computer and a child's toy with plenty of buttons to push. "Don't touch," the woman admonishes again, barely looking up. I guess she's seen this, said this, before.

I take a seat at a round table near the back. Bright plastic cloths on the 20-odd tables make the room look like a party space. Orange, green, yellow, pale blue. Some with patterns. One with yellow pears, purple grapes and red apples over a white background. I am the only one sitting.

A man in a ball cap and shorts opens the fridge. A rich scent of grapes fills the room. "Delicious," I think. "These have to be thrown out," he says. The counter woman stops him. "No they don't," she snaps, ending the conversation.

No one seems phased that there is a stranger in the room, let alone one taking notes. And no one seems to have gone to tell Pastor Gena I'm here, but she and her colleagues appear right on schedule: Gena from the main stairs, part-time pastor Steve Atkinson and student Lindsay Stewart from separate directions. Lindsay is on a placement from the George Brown College community social service worker program. She, Steve and Gena make up the staff. All the others hustling around the place are volunteers, including the kids.

Gena Torres has the look of someone at home no matter where she lands. I know from our brief conversation on the phone that she runs the place, she recently lost her husband, and her son is in hospital recovering from life-changing injuries from a motorcycle crash. But when she plunks down on the chair next to me, I'm convinced she has all the time in the world to chat. Her sentences start with "yes," always building on what's come before.

I know it's a technique of improvisational comedy, the "yes, and . . ." leading to collaboration and a stronger group outcome. Gena, I think, lives it.

The kids whiz by again, and Gena tells me they are here through an arrangement with a nearby Montessori school. As part of the curriculum, they help pack grocery bags for the food bank.

We talk about the clients the Sharing Place supports. I'm surprised that in this affluent area where semidetached houses boast million-dollar price tags there is a need. I don't get to finish the question. "Eighty percent are from around this area," Steve jumps in, with Gena finishing the thought. "The majority come from this area, but I don't believe in turning anyone away."

Some have lost a job and, until they are back on their feet, have to choose between paying the mortgage and eating, Gena says. "People going through a divorce," Steve adds, "so it's not that they don't have any money, but it's not enough to make it work."

He leans in, animated, explaining the invisible poor — in the neighbourhood, but living in a room above a store or sharing a basement. They are working but not earning enough to make ends meet. Some are ill and others are homeless.

Lindsay listens, quietly taking in the stories of her mentors. Her messy bun shifts as she nods her head. I take that to mean she recognizes the scenarios. They must be the textbook case studies.

Running a food bank, offering community meals and supporting people in need is part of the mission of the Church of the Nazarene, part of its compassionate ministry. Founded as a global ministry in 1908, its members seek to serve God through service to others. It's been at this address for more than 20 years, surrounded by two-storey brick homes owned by increasingly educated and affluent families. Twenty years ago the neighbourhood would have housed more labourers and multigenerational households. Where a corner convenience store was then, an artisanal market café serves up lattes and raw cheese. While I haven't noticed the poverty, the neighbours haven't noticed the church.

Two years ago, Gena was invited to a street party on the road that abuts the church. "People that stand out there at the bus stop every day didn't know we were here," she says, her voice rising in disbelief. "I mean, it was amazing. Like people have these blinders on and they don't see what's around them."

Picking up speed, she can't help herself from recounting the full dialogue. "People were saying, 'Where are you?' And I was saying, 'I'm just around the corner at the bus stop.' 'I take that bus every day and I've never seen the Sharing Place.' And I'm thinking, 'Well, it's right there. It could bite you.'"

I'm having similar thoughts about the fruit trees we don't see even when the sidewalks are littered with berries.

"People in the community want to be involved and

connect," Gena continues, settling down. "But if they don't know we're here, then they can't do that. I'm not against putting food in your supermarket's bin for Second Harvest or for Daily Bread [two large city food banks], but on your doorstep is a need."

We do want to help. It feels good. The UK's Mental Health Foundation says helping others promotes positive physiological changes in the brain associated with happiness. Psychologists refer to the phenomenon as "helper's high." The more technical description comes from neuroscientists. Jorge Moll and a team of neuroscience researchers working at the National Institutes of Health in Maryland used functional magnetic resonance imaging to see what happens when people anonymously donate to real charitable organizations related to major societal causes. "We show that the mesolimbic reward system is engaged by donations in the same way as when monetary rewards are obtained."

I thought I was participating in the pick for research, and I enjoy the outside activity that ends with a bag of fruit in my kitchen, but I realize I am also looking for that uplift that comes from doing good.

I ask about the grim-looking apples we brought in on Sunday night. They were pockmarked with spotted brown flesh. It's likely cork spot, a harmless but unattractive disease. What will they do with them?

Gena laughs. "Well, I don't know, because I cut one open and they are brown inside. The yellow ones that they brought in previously are good. But we're going to figure something out. We do have a few clients who have the facilities to bake." Not many, she adds.

I tell her about the pickers who planned to use them for cider, and my own default for ugly fruit: sauce or crumble.

"I don't know who's doing the cooking Thursday morning," Gena says, then suggests the apples would make a good topping for hot cereal.

I'm starting to feel like the mom who hands out live goldfish as loot bags at a child's birthday party. Lovely gesture, and now someone else has to take care of them. "What about the grapes," I push. "They smell terrific."

"Yeah, yeah," she agrees. "We'll see what we're going to do. We'll put it out with the breakfast on Thursday morning."

Volunteers are moving in and out of the room as we sit talking. They're sorting bread, moving food to the back, washing the grapes.

Maybe those unwanted fruits are an acquired taste or need a gourmet's hand to create something fabulous. Or maybe we'd be better off bringing the blossoms in the spring as a floral arrangement. Perhaps I just hit a bad tree.

Nick Saul, head of Community Food Centres Canada, is dogged in his efforts to restore dignity to charity. Working against the proverb "beggars can't be choosers" drove Saul to transform a Toronto food bank into an innovative community food centre. In his book *The Stop* he talks about putting his foot down on rejecting dented cans, wilted produce and failed or super-processed food experiments. "The food bank experience is so often a slow, painful death of the spirit — forcing yourself to visit a crowded, ill-equipped, makeshift place, answer personal questions, swallow your pride as you wait in a lineup," he writes. "Reaching the front of the line only to be offered bizarre processed food products or slimy, wilted lettuce that couldn't be revived with electric shock treatment is the final nail in the coffin."

It's not exclusively a Canadian or even North American problem. During the Milan Expo in 2015, chef Massimo Bottura put together a project to feed the hungry from left-over Expo food. We may think of Italy as a bastion of good homemade food, but even there, food is wasted while people suffer. Far from a soup kitchen, organizers built a modern, light-filled dining hall that would allow a team of high-profile chefs invited from around the world to prepare nutritious and pleasing multicourse meals. Bottura's goal was to feed the body and nourish the soul, treating each guest with dignity. There was no lining up for paper plates of mash; servers delivered meals to the table on ceramic dishes. The plan was duplicated for the Olympics in Rio de Janeiro. Among the guest chefs there was Canadian Joshna Maharaj, who had transformed Ryerson University's food services by serving fresh, local and sometimes campus-grown fruits, herbs and vegetables. In Rio, Joshna's team used rescued ingredients to make chicken curry with grilled palm hearts and a mango and passionfruit chutney. The Milan and Rio projects were so successful, so eye-opening, they continue under Bottura's nonprofit organization Food for Soul. The organization has expanded to several similar community kitchens elsewhere in Italy and in West London, with plans for more, always with an effort to engage the community in efforts to stop food waste and to consider sharing a meal, as Bottura says, "as a gesture of love."

Our gnarly apples were picked with the best intentions, but with no celebrity chef in sight, they don't add to the dignity of charity. Yet Gena says the free fruit is still welcome. Urban harvesters have brought in apples, grapes and cherries this year. Like most food banks, the bulk of what the Sharing Place packs for clients is nonperishable: canned vegetables, tuna and pasta. It's all helpful but not always the healthiest choice, Gena says. The fruit helps balance the offerings, and it's not always ugly.

"The cherries were unbelievable," Steve remembers, nudging Gena's memory.

"Yeah, the cherries were beautiful; I don't know where they got them from, but they were like 'wow.' They were gone by the end of the day."

Again, that rich scent of dark grapes blooms. Behind Lindsay, a woman with a white towel hanging around her neck picks through bunches in a large metal bowl. A gentle chime rings through the room now and again as her scissors hit the edge. As Gena, Steve and Lindsay head back to their duties, I slip over to meet Gertie French.

Gertie and her husband have been making a 45-kilometre drive from suburban Pickering twice a week for 15 years to volunteer here. "It's quite a drive in the morning, I tell you," she says, ringed fingers flashing across the gems of fruit. She comes because of the church denomination and, like many self-effacing volunteers, she insists, "It keeps us busy. It gives us something to do."

She works as she talks, snipping and sorting the fruit. "I thought I'd just take off the busted ones and clean it up for the clients," she says, "because they'll just take it and eat it and not worry if it's washed or anything."

I'd do the same, but I don't tell her that. I pop one of her grapes into my mouth and ask her if she's tried them. She joins me, and we pause like sommeliers concentrating on the flavour. Gertie offers no hints. I ask what she thinks of the taste. "It was good, yeah, it was good, very good." I have to agree.

She's splitting the grapes into small bunches and putting them in yogurt containers, easy for clients to take away.

Gena has invited me to come back for dinner on Thursday to see how our fruits are received. It's the end of the season. There won't be more. I'm hoping they don't go to waste.

Down the stairs in the dining room, Pastor Steve is in full flight. He's recapping the story of Jacob and how he was tricked into marrying Rachel's sister Leah. From behind a music-stand pulpit, he tosses out questions to the crowd. "Can you believe it? Imagine being married to your sister-in-law! The veils. Whaddaya think that means?" Lindsay waves as I come in. Like an auctioneer on a sitcom, Steve takes her gesture to mean she has an answer. More laughter. I've missed the story but not the enthusiasm. The room is energized and fully engaged. Steve slips into grace, thanking the Lord for good food. "Women first," he calls out. "No, wait, there is a child," a voice calls back. "He's upstairs," says another. The line has already formed. Women load their paper plates with salad, rolls and pasta smothered in vegetables.

I take off my damp coat and ask Steve how the fruit was received. He thinks Gena took the apples home to make sauce. It hasn't come back yet.

I recognize some of the dinner guests from the street. One is often in front of the liquor store carrying, it seems, all of his belongings. Seeing these people in a different setting changes my view. No longer a reminder of our inadequate support systems, at a table with a community in a safe place, they are diners and friends and the people who will pass the salt, if you need it.

Moving on to Lindsay, in my hunt for the fate of those ugly apples we brought, I ask if she knows if people liked them. Lindsay tells me they were a hard sell to the clients who came through the food bank last week. I feel a bit rejected. She can see it. "I told them they were OK to eat," she says, watching my face for reaction. Some were taken by a group of Spanish-speaking women and a Polish couple. They planned to make pies. They're not here tonight, so I'll come back next week to see if I can catch them. I added some of my share of the apples to a pan of pork medallions earlier tonight. Caramelized in the juices, they were a good addition to our meal.

It takes several visits over several more weeks before I find someone who tried the rusty apples. A tall man in pressed black pants and a dark dress shirt catches me as I'm working my way through the room. Alexandre Lupse came to Canada 12 years ago from Romania. The Sharing Place helped him as he got his feet on the ground. He found work in an auto glass shop and then a bakery. A workplace fall left him with two broken vertebrae in his back. As he reaches for his coffee cup, I see tremors in one arm. It may be Parkinson's disease, he tells me, maybe something else. He comes to the Sharing Place to volunteer, he says, doing whatever is needed — cleaning, vacuuming, fixing anything electrical. I ask him about the red apples from our pick and the yellow from another tree.

"*Da*, yellow is more better, more taste, red I eat only two," he tells me.

"The red had a lot of brown spots," I admit.

"Yah, but I peel . . . I cut smaller. I eat, two pieces only I take, yellow I take a lot, maybe 10 pieces, good taste, I like."

Alexandre has an apartment with a full kitchen. But now I feel a bit foolish. Some of the clients here have a room with no access to a kitchen, or they have a hotplate and maybe a microwave. It's too much work to process fruit that can't be eaten out of hand. I'm not suggesting that the people who harvest city fruit with the goal of helping the city's hungry are oblivious, but following the fruit from tree to table has reminded me that making something as simple as applesauce or cider is out of reach for many.

Months later, on a painfully hot day, volunteer pickers were disappointed with a mushy crop of cherries, past the best-before date. Val Colden was the leader on that pick too and made the decision that they couldn't be donated. It wouldn't be fair to the receiving organization. But we still had to pick them because we had promised the owner we would. We cleared the tree and I brought my soggy share home. After some head scratching, we turned them into a topping for cheesecake. We used up what would have been wasted food, but we didn't get to share the bounty. Understandably, food banks will distribute only commercially processed foods; there's no protocol for testing how safe home canning is. Chef Bottura's *refettorio* model is one option to respond to that, albeit a massive undertaking. Another could be to enlist the support of a willing commercial kitchen to process and share. Hidden Harvest in Ottawa has an informal arrangement with a local chef who turns excess elderberries into syrup. Hidden Harvest uses the jars of sweet nectar for promotions and celebrations. The next step could be another sibling charity that jars wasted food so it can be sent to food banks and other organizations that offer food to those in need.

I catch Pastor Gena before I head out the door. She tells me the grapes I carried in the cargo bike were juiced and used for communion. "That's a very special use," I prompt, thinking of the quiet but significant Christian ritual of sharing wine or juice to represent the blood of Christ and bread to represent his body.

"It is precious," Gena agrees, noting that the grapes used for the wine at the Last Supper would also have been very local. At the time, near Jerusalem, wine was often made from grapes dried on the vine and flavoured with pomegranate and spices, creating a sweet, concentrated beverage. Our neighbourhood pickers likely left wizened fruit behind, and not everyone wanted even the juicy orbs. The transformation from garbage grapes to holy wine was simple. Seeing the potential and making the transformation happen starts with believing it can be done.

COCONUT SASKATOON (SERVICEBERRY) ICE CREAM (GLUTEN-FREE, VEGAN)

The Grandview Woodland Food Connection in Vancouver works with people who are vulnerable or struggling financially. Access to good-quality food is a priority for the organization, so when the Vancouver Fruit Tree Project dropped off a box of saskatoon berries it was a welcome surprise. Community food developer Ian Marcuse says, "They are such a treat because they are not cultivated on a large scale and not often found in stores."

Ian used the berries to teach Grade 3 students at Britannia Elementary school about healthy eating with an easy two-ingredient recipe.

IAN'S VERSION

Break store-bought frozen coconut milk into chunks. Add saskatoon berries to taste. Mix the two ingredients in a good-quality blender to your desired texture.

"It was the best saskatoon berry ice cream the kids ever ate," Ian says, and a great way to end the school year.

I've revisited the recipe to suit my kitchen, tastes and not-so-good-quality blender.

INGREDIENTS

1 can full-fat coconut milk
3 teaspoons maple syrup or honey
¼ cup washed saskatoon berries

INSTRUCTIONS

1. *Shake or stir 1 can of full-fat coconut milk. Mix in 3 teaspoons of maple syrup (you can use any liquid sweetener you like). Pour into ice cube trays (1 can fits into one tray). Freeze for 2 hours until the mixture is stiff, but not rock-hard frozen.*

2. *For a single serving, transfer 6 cubes to a food processor, add ¼ cup of washed serviceberries and pulse until the mix looks like soft-serve ice cream.*

Substitute any berries you like for the saskatoons.

CHAPTER FIVE

URBAN ORCHARDS

THE COMMUNITY HEADS BACK OUTSIDE

On a walk down Oxford Street in Halifax, I was stopped by a single word hand-scrawled on masking tape wrapped around a thin tree. "Free," it read in black ink. The writer had gone over the letters to make them bolder. No other words circled the grey bark between sidewalk and road. A remnant from a garage sale, I wondered? The free item already gone? There were no signs of discounted knick-knacks scattered below. I looked up and saw instead a rogue red berry the shade of a fresh bruise. August is late for a serviceberry, one of Canada's indigenous fruits, but there it dangled, having escaped the peck of birds. Because it was planted so close to the road, I guessed it was a city tree. Urban landscapers gave the serviceberry a thumbs-up as a street tree following a 2008 study, and I've seen more of them planted in Toronto in recent years too. I don't know if the fruit was the freebie, but the sign had me thinking about how we make and share common resources.

When property is public, does it follow that anything that grows on it belongs to all of us for our use too? I found a spectacular cache of serviceberries beside a Toronto subway station in the spring. They grew in a plot beside a near-deserted automated entrance, surrounded by concrete paving, honking cars and a dusty laneway parking lot. The small patch was the only green in sight. My discovery, far from a random sprouting, had been planted in that spot with purpose. LEAF, a not-for-profit organization put them there. The full name is Local Enhancement and Appreciation of Forests, but it's a seldom-used moniker. It runs programs from Ajax to Etobicoke encouraging people to grow more trees and take care of the existing city canopy. It sells trees, plants trees and offers advice on how to keep them growing. The subway installation was one of five demonstration gardens. A large sign didn't mention a harvest. I snapped a picture and sent a tweet asking if I could pick. At this point in my city fruit hunt, I was carrying plastic containers wherever I went, so I was pleased when LEAF gave me the nod. Our youngest, still early enough in her teens to be more intrigued than embarrassed, watched me and pointed out laden branches. The fruit was perfect. One more day and it would be overripe. A woman stepped out of the back door of a medical building. Her stride slowed as she took in the scene. She looked at us skeptically and asked if the fruit was edible. I tipped my container, inviting her to taste. One berry in her mouth and her eyebrows were up. It didn't take long for her hands to reach into the trees to start her own harvest. I worried about her white blouse and passed her a spare container. Minutes later another woman arrived from the sidewalk and the same conversation followed. We picked through the trees in silence as if we were picking through the sale tables at Honest Ed's, the marquee discount emporium in its final days across the road.

I had permission; my new partners didn't need an invitation. They just followed my lead. I know picking anything in parks is not allowed, and I wouldn't think of taking fruit from a private home, but we were entering a grey area here. I have pulled fruit from trees outside office buildings. There's a terrific row of cherries, pears and apples in an industrial part of the city that I don't hesitate to pick. I have many friends who grew up harvesting berries from the wild spaces in Newfoundland and Northern Ontario. But this was the city. The idea of an urban common, an informal take-what-you-need zone, was making more sense to me.

In its medieval England version, the common was land held by the manor but open for use by tenants. It's where the term "commoner" originates, describing the unpropertied people who used it. The concept existed unnamed long before that as humans farmed, foraged and hunted on land that had no ownership. Today, it's difficult to find any unowned land, and "commons" can refer to a public square, a park or even a swimming pool, anything that is used by and for the public. The difference is, the space has some kind of management built in. So we attach rules to what you can and cannot do in a park — for example, don't pick the flowers or cut down the trees. That management or oversight evolved from what's known as the tragedy of the commons. Although the concept had been evident long before, biologist Garett Hardin popularized the term in a 1968 paper describing what happens when individuals acting in their own self-interest deplete the resources of the commons. When a farmer grazes too many sheep on common land, he might benefit, but the crops will soon be wiped out, destroying the land for grazing. If I took all of the berries on the subway bush there would be none left for other passersby, birds or insects that help feed the soil in this garden. If we were all fruit literate or even more agriculturally aware, and could tamp down our worst instincts to fill our baskets, a fruit common could work.

When Lee Herrin started his fruit-picking venture in Victoria, it was a stop-gap measure. He'd leaned on Christopher Alexander's writing from 1977. The Austrian-born architect believed a backyard tree produced too much fruit for a single family. Instead, Alexander wrote in *A Pattern Language*, we should be looking at urban orchards, common resources for anyone to harvest. "The presence of orchards adds an experience that has all but vanished from cities — the experience of growth, harvest, local sources of fresh food; walking down a city street, pulling an apple out of a tree, and biting into it." Some 20 years later, Lee, living in Victoria, was convinced but practical. Until the idea of a public orchard became real, he'd make use of the fruit that was going to waste on private property. Another 20 years on, community orchards are growing in cities around the world.

When many of us are suspicious of anyone moving across our properties and even kids don't venture through backyards uninvited, I wonder if it's the better model. That question brought me to Dartmouth, Nova Scotia, where a community had been put in charge of maintaining a public resource.

The ferry ride from Halifax to Dartmouth is quiet on a late Sunday afternoon. A couple chats in low voices a row ahead of me, windbreakers zipped up and hands cradling coffee cups. It's not a day to be on deck. Raindrops draw stripes on the windows. I seal my notebook in a plastic bag to protect it during an urban forest tour, which will include a stop at the region's first public orchard.

I meet John Simmons at the Alderney Terminal. He's the urban forester for the Halifax Regional Municipality, which includes Dartmouth. A burly guy, he's deep in discussion with David Foster, an environmental management student who works with him at the municipality. They sit backwards on the bench of a picnic table, elbows behind propping them up. They welcome me in, no formalities required. I climb over the bench opposite and ask about the Dartmouth Common orchard. From idea to shovels in the ground, it seemed to move quickly. The beauty of working in a smaller city, it turns out, is that you can get things done fast. "There are a limited number of experts internally, so those that are deemed experts have a lot of freedom," John says. And the mayor wanted action on local food production, "so there was that political direction there."

John strikes me as the kind of guy who likes it that way. Make a decision and move forward. Still, he takes the time to share his expertise and to listen, not just to me, but to others on the tour.

Two things came together to make this orchard grow. In 2013, Mayor Mike Savage held an open forum on a healthy and livable community. Local food production was on the table, and those consulted saw an urban orchard as one solution. A year earlier, others had presented the same idea in discussions for a renewed urban forest master plan. So there was chatter in the community and an interest at the political level. Agriculture was moving into the urban lexicon. Community gardens, allotment gardens and backyard sharing have become common. But a full orchard is a different thing. It's not one plot for one person, as some vegetable gardens are. It takes a bigger space, in many cases, and a few more hands to make it go.

I've heard from gardeners and foresters in Vancouver and Toronto that the idea of an orchard on public land isn't always well received. I try out the concept on John, curious about how he'd take to naysayers. "Across the country, people have found objections to urban orchards. They're messy . . ." I start.

"They are."

"They're going to attract animals . . ."

"Yeah."

"Somehow it leads to increased crime."

"Yup."

John is so matter of fact about the objections, I wonder if he's just been at it so long that nothing surprises him. Compared to other cities, Halifax seems to have had a smooth ride. John takes a sip from his travel mug and tells me political will can go a long way. He anticipated push-back and built it into the system. So when city council adopted the urban forest master plan, it gave the forester and his team all the regulatory rights they needed to move forward.

They chose a spot in Dartmouth Common, a 120-hectare stretch of land across the harbour from Halifax. The Mi'kmaq had seasonal camps in this area into the 1700s. When the British arrived, they brought the commons concept, setting aside land that was to be available for the common good. Defining that good and the meaning of a common has been open to interpretation since the beginning. It's unlikely Mi'kmaw needs were a consideration. Over the centuries the Dartmouth site has been used for private development, schools, baseball diamonds, a hotel, an armoury and burials. It also has substantial recreational greenspace, plenty of grass, trees, ball diamonds and gardens. Among other uses today, the Dartmouth Common houses an established community garden and an outdoor bake oven. That existing base of gardeners and bakers was the key to putting the orchard here.

"Stewardship plays the biggest part in these things even on the municipal line," John tells me. It's really about the ongoing costs. Cities will plant trees, but John predicts there will never be a time when Halifax will be able to fund an organization to maintain the orchards.

The woman behind Toronto's first community orchard

learned that from her city councillor early in her mission to bring fruit to her neighbourhood. Susan Poizner needed Joe Mihevc's support to plant fruit trees in a small worn-down park. "Susan, look, are you going to live here for the next five to ten years?" she remembers the councillor asking. Susan assured him she would, winning his support. Ongoing stewardship is among the first things people have to think about before they plant community trees.

Susan made it a mission to learn everything she could about fruit tree care. In fact, the former journalist and documentary maker wrote a how-to book on the subject and runs training sessions. A weekend seminar at a nursery drew a crowd of 50 gardeners, men in plaid shirts and ball caps, women in T-shirts fanning papers against the heat, middle-agers mostly with a few kids tagging along. By the end of the session they were armed with information on how to water, clean up, inspect and prune in their own backyards. In a community orchard, having one trained volunteer won't cut it. The whole community needs to know what is going on, when to pick, when to spray, how to identify diseases and how to prepare the trees for winter. And it can't just be the retirees. Susan insists every child should know how to prune and take care of a fruit tree. "Because then you've got lots of people coming up who will take care of them and harvest them and enjoy them."

A great goal, but a tall order. I think about all the things I did not learn from my parents and Anthony De Sa never burying the family fig tree. Expanding the knowledge base beyond the family tree could help connect the willing learner with the learned.

The Dartmouth Common community garden has been around for 20 years, so it made sense to put the trees nearby. There would be people already interested in growing edibles with a built-in record of passing the torch. Still, the wider community had to be consulted and informed. David Foster, John's colleague, has worked with the Sierra Club Canada Foundation and continues as a volunteer. He took on the community part of the municipality's project and was the first to feel the bumps in the road. While most people were supportive, some had objections to adding fruit to the park.

Susan discovered the same in Toronto. The city councillor had heard some rumblings, and called a community meeting. It didn't go well. "We had the meeting. There was a lot of anger. There was a lot of fear, a lot of concerns. It wasn't a pretty . . . it was kind of horrible." Susan was still shaking her head at the memory. "Other concerns that came out in the meeting were, for instance, 'My children will get cherry stains on their T-shirts.'"

Another objector, Susan told me, believed that rapes and murders would increase. "Because, you know, rapists can hide behind the trees or something like that." Yet another was worried about more roadkill because raccoons would be attracted to the fruit and then get run over on the street.

She also heard worries about bees and mess and maintenance, reasonable issues to raise, she remembered, that could be addressed with a strong and committed stewardship program.

Malcolm Bromley, Vancouver's general manager of parks and recreation, has heard similar talk; concerns about new urban orchards know no boundaries. I met Malcolm at a national park summit. His assessment is that a lot of the worries about mess come from a fixation on neatness. "If you look at British parks and British gardens, they tend to be very ornamental and very perfect in kind of how they're laid out."

We aren't meant to engage with what lies beyond the fencing. These are gardens for admiring only. Picture Kew Gardens in London or the Tuileries Garden in Paris. Parts of Dartmouth Common would fit into that picture. Park space in the common has included groomed gardens and mown grass. That European model has seeped into parks maintenance standards. Trees that drop fruit pose a conflict to the manicured approach not just for park users, but for the people who maintain them. Speed, cleanliness and mowing are the keys. "And if there are apples there, what do we do with them?" Malcolm goes to the nut of the issue: "It's helping parks people understand that the benefits far outweigh the risks."

The city's food strategy called for an increase in food assets by 50 percent between 2010 and 2020. Among those assets are community orchards. Vancouver has several urban orchards established in parks, at a golf course and on a city boulevard, with plans for more.

Vancouver is one of a growing list of North American cities now setting policy around food that grows. Karen Landman has seen the shift. She's been studying urban agriculture for 20 years and is a professor at the University of Guelph's School of Environmental Design and Rural Development. Karen says we haven't seen that kind of government involvement in urban agriculture since WWII, when people were encouraged to plant victory gardens. When the war ended, we saw the introduction of zoning bylaws, with cities laying out the rules of land use throughout municipalities. I think of my childhood neighbourhood. Houses with an expanse of lawn at the front and a tasteful display of petunias were the norm. Francesco's son was embarrassed at his father's break from that pattern. Karen says that that 1950s shift pushed agriculture out into rural areas. Now, she says, growing food within city boundaries is back on the agenda at city halls. "Increasingly now [cities] realize they have to set policies not only to regulate it but also to empower their planners and municipal staff to make sure that it happens within the urban environment."

Karen remembers the common theme of interview responses to research undertaken by one of her students. Any kind of urban agriculture has to look nice so people surrounding the site are accepting of it. "Whether it's messy on the inside, around the outside you're ringing it with beautiful flowers and lots of sunflowers and things that people enjoy. Then it becomes an amenity." And despite the backlash that Malcolm and others have heard, Karen says academic research shows community gardens increase real estate values. Free fruit could be just the beginning of the windfall.

Fifteen of us gather for the tour in Dartmouth. Among the group are the key players in the orchard project — a landscape architect, urban forest experts and others who work with the environment. Add the rest and it's not a bad turnout in the rain. John starts with a nod to the curated space where we stand at Alderney Landing on the waterfront. His orange utility jacket glares against the wet deck as he points across the plaza. We turn to look at a tall leafless tree with a crow posing on the top branch like an omen. Apparently birds love dead trees because the dried-out branches are more stable. The tree is an Austrian pine, an import. John takes a jab at the book-learning designers who work with non-native species that don't fit into the seven-thousand-year-old Canadian eco-system. So the theme of the tour has been set. We pause while a train pulling graffiti-covered rail cars passes through. Our forester barrels across the road and uphill to stop at trees I wouldn't have given any notice. He points out their features, why they were planted here and what's happened to the scruffy ones. He carries on, answering questions, jacket open to the dampness. We move along crooked sidewalks and angled roads, hoods up. A half hour in, the clouds thicken and the crackling drumbeat on my umbrella blocks John's voice. We get into the green of the commons and trudge through sodden grass. I'm watching for the rows of apple trees that to some seem so intrusive. We must be getting close, but I've seen no sign of an orchard. We stop near the outdoor bake oven, and John, wiping the water from his glasses, gestures around the area, pointing to saplings and something up the steep hill. I move closer and hear him talking about the orchard. We're in it. It's so well integrated into the space, I couldn't see it. That's not by chance.

John brought Stephen Cushing into the venture to design the orchard. As we break off the tour to amble toward the blueberries, I tell Stephen I would have walked right through, had John not pointed out the orchard trees — two peaches beside a bench, a couple of cherries and pears in the rose garden. Butternut and walnut trees are at the top of the hill, and three little pecan trees are hidden in the woods while they incubate. "No straight lines, no rows," Stephen says, smiling. "The main reason for that is there are other competing objectives in this park."

Soccer is one of them, so open spaces are important to preserve. The upside is there is plenty of sun. And when we look back at all the uses of the common over the years, the curated gardens left a positive legacy too.

As a student, Stephen had a job planting flowers here in raised beds along a sloped walkway. The planting was abandoned years ago and replaced with sod, but Stephen, now a landscape designer, knew that even a decade later, the soil would be good. He put the blueberries there — all of them hidden in plain sight.

I follow the crowd, climb up to the blueberry beds and look for the darkest specimens. A few days ago, I picked up a pint box of blueberries from the large farmers' market at Halifax's seaport. It's the oldest continuous market of its kind in North America, established by royal decree in 1750, and a popular spot on a Saturday morning. The place was crowded with tourists and locals, cotton bags and backpacks slung over shoulders getting heavier as the morning passed. A woman selling blueberries assured me, a little brusquely, that they came straight from the farm. These ones in Dartmouth Common will be straight from the bush. We've churned up the wet soil, scrambling through the garden, and now it smells like spring. The rain has washed the fruit clean. There aren't many berries, so it turns into a polite treasure hunt, each of us holding back to ensure everyone finds a fruit to sample. The plants are still tagged, they're so new. That's the beauty of most berries. They offer instant gratification, fruiting immediately, while the trees could take a decade before they are ready for a full harvest. Plump green berries cover the plants almost to hip level. Almost two dozen fill a single cluster. An animal has chewed through a few leaves. The pointed ovals are shiny and bright with the wetness, making them even more robust looking. I find a ripe berry low in the bush, matte blue, almost grey. I pull from the stem and it gives easily. Full flavour bursts into my mouth through the pop of the broken skin. Wild berries tend to have a more dynamic flavour. These are a pretty close second. Maybe it's the rain and the atmosphere. Perhaps it's the difference between several seconds and several hours off the plant.

It's a good place to wind up the tour. The conversations turn to questions about litter and vandalism and who's picking. A woman in a blue slicker mentions the effects of Hurricane Juan. The 2003 storm wiped out a lot of trees. But the silver lining is room for brambles and a surge in raspberry canes. The new orchard includes raspberries and haskap berries, another blueberry-like fruit that has a Japanese and Russian heritage. There has been a surge in interest in haskaps after researchers started breeding and developing the crop in the 2000s. University of Saskatchewan professor Bob Bors is credited with a lot of that work. He heads the university's fruit program. Propagators across Canada sell varieties developed through the program. Among them is Lehave Forests in Nova Scotia.

Someone mentions kids foraging here a few days ago. David Foster, the Sierra Club connection, is encouraged. It's exactly the benefit he'd hoped to see. "Anybody can come in here anytime, pick however much they want, enjoy it, they can bake something with it, they can share it with their friends."

Free food is the first benefit. Foster hopes those casual pickers bring their friends and family to make this a gathering place to eat, talk about food security and "just be a community." Then maybe they'll be encouraged to plant a tree in their own backyard, he says. We'll have come full circle. From first immigrants planting orchards for settlers to private trees in backyards, to volunteers repurposing those trees and now to architects and foresters establishing urban orchards, he sees the community going back behind the fence.

Once the trees were planted, the volunteer gardeners took over the maintenance. It will be another decade before the orchard produces a substantial crop. John figures he'll have retired by then. The next phase — using the output (however you define it) — belongs to a different city department, recreation. John pictures lectures on shrubs and trees, a how-to-pick-fruit session or a canning workshop. It's part of connecting people with food, the environment and each other. It's also what many of the urban harvesters have done.

Those are high expectations for a few fruit trees. I try to find a parallel. One of my neighbours organizes a several-blocks-long street sale each spring. No one makes much money out of it, and I'm pretty sure we're cycling a lot of stuff through the same households. But it's a morning when everyone is outside, sharing stories about how to get value out of a fondue set and getting to know not just the people next door, but the folks on the next block. So, yes, it builds community. You might find a lamp that fits into your decor or a book you've meant to read. It doesn't matter. It's not about the stuff. In the community orchard, it's not about the food. More than half of the world's population lives in urban environments. It's a huge and rapid shift; the United Nations estimates that by 2030, five billion of us will live in cities and towns. That means less access to wandering through farmland. Even today, for many of us, it's not a simple thing to get to a place where food grows. The orchard will not create food security, but it can address a social inequity. While John, David and Stephen may be able to get away for a weekend of camping or take a drive into the countryside from time to time, for many, personal finances make that unlikely. Orchards like the one in Dartmouth Common may be the best or only platform some have to garden and see how food grows. So education and access to agriculture also matter.

That's right up David's alley. "I like the idea of spreading the importance of coming back to the environment, especially in our cities because realistically that's where we're going to encounter it the most." There are spectacular parks in Nova Scotia, including Kejimkujik National Park, but those who can get to them might do so two weekends in a year, maybe go for a week-long trip at best. Meanwhile, city dwellers can be connected to urban parks like the Dartmouth or Halifax Common or Point Pleasant every day. "We need to have a little bit more of an interaction with nature on a daily basis."

Back at Ben Nobleman Park in Toronto, Susan Poizner had similar discussions about the benefits of installing an orchard. The park is across the street from the site of a new subway tunnel expansion. Huge equipment bored a path deep underneath the layers of asphalt, roads, sewers and cables that keep the modern city running. It's loud work. And ugly-dirty. We'll all use the line when it's built, of course, but in the meantime, it's a mess.

I was taking in the scent of a particularly fragrant blossom when Susan arrived, tall and slim, a red embroidered bag bouncing off a hip as she strolled into the park. It's not a big space but it's an oasis of green. The racket of ambulance sirens and jackhammers were slightly muffled by new leaves, and I could hear birdsong in the trees. Getting to this point wasn't a smooth ride. Susan has lived in the neighbourhood for 15 years. She said the park used to be empty. No one came. "It was scuzzy; there was a horrible playground. It was just a creepy place."

The visionaries believed it could be much more. Susan introduced me to the trees that are making it so. "These are our two newest babies. Two Asian pears and a cherry. We just watered them yesterday." She pointed to a small growth with not many signs of life. "This is starting to blossom too."

"And that's enough, eh? Those two little blossoms? That makes you happy?"

"Oh, it makes me happy they're going to blossom fully. At least I know it's alive. You get the bare root tree, it could be dead as far as you know, right? So, this cutie little cherry . . ."

It was cute, as far as plants go. It was a cherry bush they were experimenting with.

An airplane whined overhead, adding to the cacophony of construction. The park was deserted on a weekday afternoon. Naptime is the best time to come to a playground, if you don't like crowds. All the swings are free, no one is crying and you can use as much of the picnic table as you like. We settled into the long harvest table. Made from 13 pieces of solid pine reclaimed from Toronto's first docks, the table is part of what the orchard has brought to the neighbourhood. The docks had been buried, covered with landfill, more than one hundred years ago as the city built south into the water. When excavators digging for a new development uncovered the treasure, the pieces were up for grabs. We don't routinely find wood cut in long lengths anymore. This table sits 20.

The organization that grew around the Ben Nobleman orchard brought the table in. The first person to use it was one of the early opponents of the orchard. She hosted a children's birthday party in the park, balloons and all. Susan ran a hand over the wood, pleased with the memory of the change from foe to friend. It's what the orchard was meant to do. "For me it's about making greenspace interactive. It's about animating the space as well as feeding ourselves. It's about being creative."

I wondered about the dynamic between the naysayers and the proponents as they meet in the park now. Susan has no hard feelings. In some ways, she said, the opponents were right. "We didn't know how to care for them, even though we were gardeners. We didn't know how to prune them. We knew nothing about pests and disease and how to prevent it. So in a way, they gave us a huge gift, because we could not mess up."

To avoid "I told you so," she hit the books, called experts, ran workshops and learned.

Then there was the assumption on the part of the organizers, Susan included, that fruit trees are easy to grow. They'd just put them in the ground and they'd be beautiful with their blossoms and shade, they'd produce fruit and they'd come back each year. The organizers lost a lot of trees until they trained up on pruning, organic spraying and managing disease. It happens. The trick is knowing how to deal with disease quickly to protect the rest of the crop. The group had wanted 40 trees. In a compromise, they got 14.

A sparrow chirped above our heads and then something fell behind me, loud enough to distract us. The bird had dropped a scrap of garbage, in error perhaps or as a deliberate warning to us. No matter, as we were soon distracted by the distinctive din of a class trip: the high voices of children, excited about being outside, released from the labours of the classroom. They stood at the edge of the park, like horses at the gate until their teacher freed them with final instructions. Then they were off, racing, pink, purple and blue blurs above Velcro runners, not to the swing set but the trees.

"Miss Yu, come over here! Miss Yu!"

"The weeds are not letting my tree grow."

"The weeds are not letting . . . but they're all friends, buddy. They're all friends." Miss Yu is sympathetic. "The dandelions are actually not that bad."

Susan was overwhelmed with emotion. "Oh my gosh, this is so great." She loved that the kids referred to the trees as "mine."

Two students, one ponytailed in pink, the other in orange, clutching notebooks and pencils, plunked down at the base of an apple tree to draw what they saw. Miss Yu encouraged them to get up close, feel the bark and smell it. They'd been here in the fall, selected a tree to sketch and were disappointed when they returned a week later to find no change. But on this day, there were buds and some blossoms.

Perpetual motion filled the park as Susan and the teacher exchanged notes and made plans to reconnect.

"We planted the fruit trees and all of a sudden the atmosphere changed," Susan, in full grin, told Miss Yu.

"That's so wonderful. Thank you for doing it. It's amazing."

"It's the trees, you know. They're the ones that bring this gorgeous energy into the park."

Susan saw an opening to put in a pitch for fruit literacy. Without accusing kids, she told the teacher about how the apples were harvested before they were ripe. It was a waste and a frustrating moment for the people who worked to nurture them to maturity. To be fair, how would someone who has never picked fruit from a tree know? I've had those moments with tropical fruits in the grocery store. When is a mango ready to eat? Or a dragon fruit? I've asked one of the checkout clerks, who told me she's from the Caribbean. She just laughed and said they are never ripe here, meaning in a northern climate grocery store.

To help bring that literacy along, the Ben Nobleman crew is looking at signage or some physical symbol to let people know when it's OK to pick. That turns me to rules. What kind of rules does a community orchard have, with great goals of being free for all? When I put that question to the folks in Halifax, even the government workers said there aren't any rules. Susan turned to Boston and a now-defunct group called EarthWorks. It was among the first to plant community orchards in the '70s. She asked one of the players what the group did if people stripped the trees and took all the fruit for themselves. "He said that means we need to plant more fruit trees. And I thought that's beautiful."

A beautiful thought, yes. But in practice, Susan wasn't

so pleased. "How did I feel the first time somebody stripped one of our fruit trees? I was pretty grumpy."

As a result, she thinks some rules are OK. That means signs that say something like "feel free to harvest one or two fruits but leave some behind for others to pick." It's a question that dogs all community orchard groups. The thought that I had overpicked the subway serviceberries was on my mind. Perhaps a few rules would make picking easier. A friend in Northern Ontario describes blueberry picking as synonymous with summer. Northerners head to the bush as soon as the fruit is ripe and pick the shrubs clean. I hear the same from Newfoundland, where the berries are so abundant you can fill a mason jar from no more than an arm's length away. To the last generation, that was the way to go. If you left any behind it meant the next picker would have to travel farther to get enough for the winter.

These city trees aren't old Newfoundland. They're not big enough to harvest for a pantry full of preserves. Just as the big box store created a new form of gluttony, I wonder if access to abundance in nature makes us over-consume. I'm not the first to ponder this.

Susan and her Orchard People company are among the founders of the Community Orchard Network. It's a virtual space to share experiences, ideas and ask questions about setting up and maintaining orchards in cities. She told me one of the newer members was a woman from Portugal looking for guidance on setting up a community orchard in Lisbon. I was stunned. What would Anthony De Sa's uncle David and Gabriel, the fellow from Madeira we met on the Lost Rivers tour, make of that? Here I am tracking the fruit footprint of Portuguese and other European immigrants in Canadian cities, the experts who can grow anything, the people who figured out burying a fig tree would keep it growing, and in Lisbon people don't know how to grow a fruit tree? I have heard that many immigrants become stuck in time when they leave their homeland. The language doesn't evolve as it would where everyone speaks it. Traditions become precious and thus preserved. My father had visions of an impoverished rural Ireland long after his brothers had a television and telephone installed in the old farmhouse. Portugal, of course, has changed from the '50s, when a large migration came to Canada. The same loss of interest in and knowledge about fruit trees has hit its cities. Moirika Reker wanted to change that. She's a visual artist, a researcher on the garden, the city and the landscape at the University of Lisbon and a self-described "would-be gardener." With a group of like-minded pomiculturalists, she's working to set up a community orchard in a Lisbon park. On her organization's Pick Your Own (City) Fruit website, she describes the first steps. They needed funding, municipal support and land. They settled on Quinta dos Lilases because when it was private property, there had been an orchard. When it became a public park the fruit trees were replaced with ornamental varieties.

"All over Portugal there are fruit trees planted in parks and streets, but those are mainly bitter, sour, or ornamental varieties, planted just for their beauty," the manifesto reads. "Our aim is to have as many edible fruits planted as we can, and gradually show that picking your own fruit and sharing free food, are great ways to actively engage with the public space. After all, it's our city, our streets, our food!"

The group talks about community building, food security and appropriation of public space. Across oceans, we are discussing the same things, inventing the same models of public access to city fruit as a means of engagement.

Moirika travelled to Finland and Poland in 2015 to see how urban orchardists there are managing. It seems concerns about overpicking aren't unique to North America. One of the main gripes she's heard about public fruit relates to stealing. "Won't people steal the fruits? Isn't it all taken away as soon as it ripens? Am I going to work for months in a row to water and protect a tree for someone to come along and steal it?"

In Helsinki, where there is a well-established urban agriculture ethos, she heard that, "as people see the public space as theirs, it makes no sense for them to vandalize it or to spoil it, let alone steal." In fact, she wrote, "steal" is the wrong word; taking a few pieces of fruit is what's expected.

In Poland, Moirika headed to a recovered Warsaw orchard. The site had belonged to the military, then became a public park. People working to protect the area's meadows found old apple trees in a heavily treed section of the park. Fruit tree advocates pruned and trimmed them and cleared out some invasive trees. They added a few fruit bushes and made plans to bring in the community.

These are far from the first or only models of urban orchards around the globe. They've popped up throughout the United States in Philadelphia, Berkeley and Los Angeles and in Wellington, New Zealand. The mother lode is in England, a country with a long reverence for the apple. For the backstory, I turned to *The Apple Source Book*, by Sue Clifford and Angela King, two of the founders of Common Ground. The group, which examines the relationship between nature and culture, first put forward the idea of community orchards in the UK in 1992, and since then, many have been recovered or planted. "In city, suburb or village, the Community Orchard is becoming the equivalent of local woodland a century or more ago — a communal asset for the parish," they wrote, making the case for the orchard as the focal point for improved diet and physical activity and quicker recovery of the sick. They quote James Crowden's words from *Cider — The Forgotten Miracle*.

"It is perhaps through trees, and orchards in particular, that we convey our sense of permanence in an otherwise largely impermanent world, and at the same time there is blossom, fruit, juice, beverage, even spirit, and firewood . . ."

These orchards around the world have started a

discussion and created communities of like-minded people. The backyard tree may produce too much fruit for today's family, as Christopher Alexander predicted, but all of the orchard people I spoke to said there is room and a need for both models. Neither can do all things, but both add to fruit and food literacy. I think about moving our serviceberry to the front yard, where there's more sun. And when I've had my fill, I'll tape a note to the trunk that says "Free."

BLUEBERRY CRISP

When Hurricane Juan hit Nova Scotia in 2003, shutting down
roads and cutting off supplies, restauranteur Lil MacPherson
thought about climate change and how much we depend
on shipped-in food. The result was the Wooden Monkey, a
Halifax restaurant that strives to support and help grow a
healthier, local, sustainable food system in Nova Scotia.
The Monkey's Dartmouth location is a short walk from the
Dartmouth Common. This large-batch recipe comes courtesy
of the Wooden Monkey kitchen.

INGREDIENTS (FILLING)

9 cups blueberries
1 cup organic cane sugar
2 tbsp arrowroot (or organic non-GMO cornstarch)
4 tbsp water
½ juiced lemon

INGREDIENTS (TOPPING)

¼ cup sesame seeds
½ cup organic spelt flour
1 ½ cups organic oats
¼ cup oil, (non-GMO) canola, sunflower, or safflower
¼ cup maple syrup

INSTRUCTIONS

1. *Combine in a saucepan blueberries, sugar, and lemon. Bring to a boil then reduce heat to a simmer, cooking until mixture thickens.*
2. *Mix together arrowroot flour and water.*
3. *Turn off heat and stir in arrowroot mixture.*
4. *Pour into desired baking dish (mixture does freeze well).*
5. *Mix together crumb topping, top prepared pan.*
6. *Bake at 350°F until top is browned, serve with vanilla ice cream or maple whipped cream, if desired.*
7. *Make a big cup of tea and enjoy!*

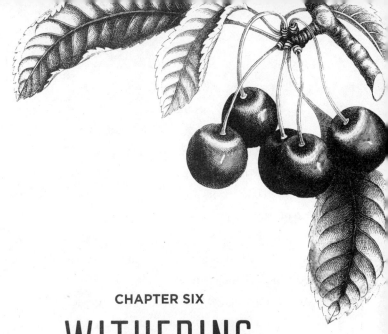

CHAPTER SIX

WITHERING ON THE VINE

THE SLIDE TO FOOD ILLITERACY

"What is a recipe?"

Mojgan Fay puts the question to a sold-out room of people gathered for the Culinary Historians of Canada's annual Mad for Marmalade event.

"Something that is passed down," one woman offers.

"It comes from the Latin word 'to receive,'" says another.

"It's a story."

"An invitation to taste something you haven't tasted before . . . letting you in."

"It's a map into your memory and experience."

"It's a history of my family and culture."

"It's a bridge from your past, present and future."

Mojgan is overwhelmed. She wrote a master's thesis in communications and culture on the subject, starting not as a foodie but as a young woman from Iran coming to terms with her identity. Exploring that through food, and how recipes move from household to household, generation to generation, connected her with the past.

She tells the group where she began: "I thought a recipe was a list of ingredients." The audience cracks up.

I laugh too, but I might have answered the same until a few years ago. When my parents died, the recipes left behind became precious. Emptying the kitchen, holding the tools my mom had held in her hands so often was difficult. My two sisters and I each took something as a working keepsake: a big brown ceramic mixing bowl, unglazed around the rim so cooks could rap a spoon clean

— our mom used it for everything from muffin batter to turkey dressing; a wooden rolling pin, missing a handle and shiny from smoothing out decades of cookie dough; a glass fruit bowl that held nothing more exotic than oranges and bananas. Opening the recipe drawer — too many bits and pieces for one of those tidy boxes other moms had — felt like we were reading our mother's diary. Handwritten margin notes, oily stains reminding us of how often they were followed and the carefully scripted cursive she used to copy a neighbour's cheesecake instructions evoked all of the feelings described by the people eager to share with Mojgan. We kept the best of them, bound them into a book and made copies for each of us and our children.

That we need a mixing bowl implies use of a recipe, even if it's just a few ingredients. Although humans have always been omnivores, it's difficult to know when we started combining foods. One of the few records we have of concoctions of edibles comes from early recipes, etched in cuneiform tablets thousands of years ago. One of the earliest Mesopotamian recipes was for a broth. In 1140, scribes at England's Durham Cathedral monastery jotted down cooking instructions in Latin. Those medieval recipes were intended to improve health or cure ailments. They must have thought it was information at risk of being forgotten. We haven't stopped producing cookbooks, but whoever instructed the scribes was right: we've forgotten a lot.

I turned to the Culinary Historians to find out when

our slide to food and fruit illiteracy began. The historians' annual winter celebration of all things citrus coincides with Seville orange season. This day is themed around the flavours of the Persian kitchen. One hundred enthusiastic men and women huddle around white-linened tables. Oranges, limes and yellow daisies add scent to the centrepieces. Melon-coloured spatulas poke out of narrow empty shot glasses, and mason jars for water sit ready for palate cleansing.

The plenary session is in the "blue barracks" (only the doors are blue) at Fort York, protector of Upper Canada and a key target during the War of 1812. Archeologists found shards of marmalade pots here, a clue to the soldiers' diet so long ago, so it's an apt place to celebrate the confection. History animators dressed in period costume rush in and out of the kitchen. The room includes chefs, home cooks and historians who follow history and culture through food. They greet food writers Naomi Duguid and Elizabeth Baird with wild applause and they jockey for position at the buffet table to capture images of the mounds of Persian meatballs and jewelled rice. They are really into food.

They're not typical. Despite the number of food celebrities gaining stature, most of us don't spend much time in the kitchen, let alone in the backyard growing a fruit tree. I find Fiona Lucas, head of the Culinary Historians of Canada, for another perspective. She has devoted a career to collecting, preserving, researching and writing about food. I ask her when we started to lose our knowledge of how food gets to the table.

"Definitely postwar. The '50s, '60s," she says. Modern conveniences meant options. And making your own bread, cakes and preserves seemed old-fashioned. All of those chores had been arduous, and women were happy to ditch them. "Look at the supermarkets. You could literally walk in, walk out with everything, without doing it yourself. So that process, once it started, was really fast."

Refrigerators with larger freezers, designed for more than ice cubes, also meant more room to keep food longer and less need for buying fresh food daily. Around 1950, careers in ice cutting disappeared. The long toothy saws are in museums now (and the movie *Frozen*). The number of cars in Canada went from roughly 1.5 million in 1945 to 2.6 million in 1950. We could move farther afield and find more property, new houses and room for a garage and driveway in the suburbs. We could fill the trunk with groceries for a week. No need for daily trips to the market. In many cases, orchards were bulldozed to make way for new subdivisions. In Mississauga, just west of Toronto, developers bought hundreds of acres of apple orchards and renamed part of the community of Dixie to Applewood. They kept some of the trees intact, timing the 1951 gala opening for when the blossoms would be in full show.

Thomas Kennedy was Ontario's prime minister (as the leader of the province was known in those days) from 1948–49 and was a lifelong fruit grower from Dixie. He had served as minister of agriculture in the '30s and '40s. In *Dixie: Orchards to Industry*, Kathleen Hicks writes that Kennedy was a huge supporter of farm life, but not one to mourn the good old days. "I wouldn't want to go back to them. They were too hard and modern living is so comfortable."

So comfortable that we stopped needing to spray and prune and could enjoy the blossoms while eating our store-bought apples. Then we forgot what those blossoms would bring and eventually, for many of us, whether the fruit growing in our own neighbourhoods was safe to eat.

In Winnipeg, home economist Getty Stewart remembers finding white blossoms among bushes she was clearing in the backyard of her new home not so long ago. When she figured out it was a Nanking cherry bush, she harvested, much to the concern of her neighbours who were convinced the fruit was poisonous. Getty also saw bags of apples ready for the garbage curbside in the fall. It was the prompt in 2010 to start Fruit Share, Winnipeg's urban harvest organization.

"It's such a shame and such a waste," she says, sad for the people who toss their fruit, not fully able to appreciate their own backyards.

Like Fiona Lucas, Getty says the drift from recognizing the value of fruit began postwar, "when we became enamoured with processed foods and it became a status symbol that 'I don't need to do this because I have Kraft on my side.'"

The convenience factor hit harder in the '70s, with more dual-income households and less time to cook. More advertising encouraged us to simplify our busy lives. Because we could purchase ready-made food, teaching our children to cook could be limited to open, heat, serve. My mother was at home with us, but she did not put anything up for the winter. No jars of preserves or homemade bread. To be fair, she grew up in an apartment, raised with her brothers by an aunt with a full-time job. Kraft did play a large role in our kitchen, and we were once treated to an "apple" pie made from Ritz crackers; there were no apples in the recipe. So convenient. I remember being intrigued by the shelves of full mason jars that lined the basement stairs in a neighbour's house. I wasn't sure what they were for. But my mom cooked a lot — takeout was limited to a pizza from time to time — and so did we. All four kids were welcome to experiment in the kitchen.

I look at Mojgan, in her twenties, among the youngest in the room, trying to find herself through recipes and see that the interest in recapturing that knowledge is there. As an extension of her thesis, Mojgan is travelling across Canada, cooking a recipe with a grandmother in each region of the country. Mojgan's session making *ghormeh sabzi*, a dried lime herb stew, with Iranian grandmothers in Toronto showed her a lot about how the recipe had been adapted over the years and across oceans. Some call it Iran's national dish and believe it can be traced back thousands of years. The grandmothers chose the recipe because it is traditional. But they'd messed with it. They used tomato paste in place of the costly saffron. They used coconut oil instead of ghee for health reasons (although the public debate about which is better continues) and tossed in some unripe grapes to add a sour tang. Mojgan looks up from her notes and pauses before telling us what these women have added to the top of this ancient dish: French fries. There are many guesses about what the iconic junk food is replacing — fried onions, slivered eggplant — but they are all wrong. The reason for the fries is simple, Mojgan says. "People like it."

Ghormeh sabzi is sometimes served with *tahdig*: rice or vegetables crisped in the bottom of a pot. I can see how tossing on some fries would be faster. It's an evolution of a recipe, but in the process of adding the convenient and popular food, they are taking the recipe one more step away from the farm and another step away from how their grandmothers taught them to make it.

While Mojgan was exploring, she was learning and reacquainting herself with the kitchen and food preparation. Many of us could stand to do the same. The growth of fast and processed foods from the '60s on, while convenient, fed food illiteracy. What's followed is a jump in type 2 diabetes, high blood pressure and heart disease. In 1970, the overall obesity rate was 9.7 percent in Canada. It hit 14.9 percent in 1998 and soared to 25.8 percent by 2015. We're not alone. An Organisaton for Economic Co-operation and Development report shows more than one in two adults and nearly one in six children are overweight or obese among its member nations, with a continuing increase.

Improving food literacy has become a full-time job for Mary Carver. Mary is the driving force behind the Ontario Home Economists' efforts to reintroduce mandatory food and nutrition classes to schools. The group has collected almost four thousand signatures on a petition to bring back food education. In addition, the 2017 Ontario Food and Nutrition Strategy, developed in consultation with more than 25 partner organizations, includes food literacy and skills as a strategic direction. Yet there is still no mandatory food literacy class for students. Fruit illiteracy is a slice of the same pie. Mary considers the cause to be a combination of missing skills and knowledge, background, lack of interest and always not enough time.

"People tend to lack food skills because they are no longer passed along from grandparent and parent," Mary says, adding that they also lack nutrition skills. Since 1942, the federal government has offered *Canada's Food Guide* as the benchmark for nutritious eating. When WWII was underway, Canadians rationed food, and the guide was developed to prevent nutritional deficiencies. It's been redesigned and adjusted over the years but not enough for an increasingly active group of experts in the medical, dietary and academic fields. Many of them argue it hasn't kept up with current research. In 2015, Health Canada announced a review of the evidence base for the guide. In the meantime, Mary says, it's our best national document for advice, the best choice for our human consumption. "There's so much information out there that's inaccurate or is not credible, is not science-based, that so many consumers are very, very confused."

What's to Eat, a Conference Board of Canada report, was funded by large food corporations, governments and the Heart and Stroke Foundation. It looked at why food literacy matters and how it could be improved. Authors Allison Howard and Jessica Brichta point to *Canada's Food Guide* as a document that has helped a lot of people improve their eating habits, but when they looked at studies that track fruit and vegetable consumption, it seemed that some of us don't follow the recommendations — in particular, men, those without postsecondary education and smokers.

What's to Eat raised concerns about the low percentage of children and adolescents who regularly participate in family meal preparation. When you open boxes for dinner, children don't have much involvement in food preparation. Future generations, the authors warn, may have even worse cooking skills.

As a freelance writer, I have been home as our girls have grown up. It hasn't been too difficult to prepare dinner at lunchtime to stew through the afternoon. I know it's a privileged position; it's increasingly difficult to run a household on one income or to put careers on hold. I hope I've prepared my kids well to identify the size of a serving, the elements of a healthy meal and why vegetables and fruit trump just about everything.

Understanding food waste can't be discounted either. Mary grew up on an apple farm, where her parents ingrained in the kids the importance of not wasting food. She scoffs at the idea of going to a big box store looking for a bulk bargain. If you can't eat three heads of romaine lettuce before they turn into a sodden mess, you haven't saved any money and you've added to the food waste problem. Successful marketing has convinced us we can buy big and save.

It's "disgusting," Mary says. "They've been caught up in this volume buying with the free parking. That's great when you're buying toilet paper." For perishable food, not so great. Knowing the impact of tossing food can fuel food literacy. So can putting your hands on ingredients with someone who's done it before. Getting a grip on what you can do with bruised peaches (smoothies, chutney, crumble), for example, makes you rethink throwing them out.

The consequences of having a poor understanding of nutrition and cooking are clear. If we can't learn it from our parents, the home economists want us to learn it in school. Home economics was mandatory for many years, as was industrial arts (most students just called it "shop"). In the '60s, students made full meals in class, doing everything from washing, chopping, kneading and buttering to baking, setting the table and cleaning up. The teacher let us use sharp knives and boiling water before we'd hit our teens. There are still such courses on the curriculum — they've been rebranded as family studies — but they aren't mandatory. And with so many other options, all interesting and valuable, Mary concedes, fewer students choose culinary life skills.

We can turn this around. That think tanks and home economists are talking about food illiteracy is reason to hope that we can be saved from the consequences of our ignorance. In 2013, the word "food" was added to the name of the Canada Agriculture and Food Museum to make a better connection between farm and fork. The museum started a food literacy program at the same time that includes canning workshops and an exhibition of the science of food preservation. We know that people preserved food thousands of years ago, stored goods deep underground in cool dark caves, precursors to the fruit cellar. They didn't know why it worked, just that it worked. Eventually, science caught up, figuring out the why, as well as better ways to keep food longer, avoiding more risk of spoiling. In 2015, the Ontario Federation of Agriculture launched a program called Six by Sixteen that aims to teach young people how to prepare six healthy locally sourced meals by the time they turn 16. Individual teachers are bringing food skills into the classroom and the classroom out into the garden. There are efforts being made, although there is no requirement for hands on knives yet.

In the blue barracks, surrounded by people chatting in intricate detail about how to use a Seville, Fiona Lucas sees positive signs. In nine years, Mad for Marmalade has grown from a small workshop to a sold-out annual event attracting some high-calibre canners. In the last few decades, she says, many people have changed their thinking about cooking. "As long as it's not about survival, making your own bread, making your own pickles, making your own preserves is wonderful. We love doing it."

Planting backyard or balcony fruits and vegetables, foraging, or picking from your neighbour's fruit tree is becoming more common. "It never disappeared but it shrank to such a small portion of daily life," Fiona says. "Now it's really reviving and it's exciting to see." She is surrounded by people who pay attention to food, who grow their own, read labels and preserve. Knowledge is growing, but we are nowhere near out of the woods.

We can see interest through the increase in preserving workshops and through the surge in organic and natural food stores. Many of us are pausing to think about what we eat and where our food comes from. Getty Stewart runs workshops across Manitoba for nonprofit organizations and other groups looking to boost food literacy. One of the province's health regions hired her to do a series of canning workshops through Southern Manitoba. She thought that in rural areas at least, the knowledge would be there. But people came out to learn more. People who have been canning and preserving all through their lives want to know the latest. Others whose parents hadn't taught them anything about putting up fruit are keenly interested. "Fruit is a gateway," she says. "It's a tasty way for me to get people interested in food and nutrition."

Why we don't cook the way generations before us did — when they had no choice, to be fair — in many cases comes down to a lack of knowledge: knowledge of ingredients, nutrition and what can be cooked fast and on a budget.

A side effect of this lack of knowledge is fear. Later in the week I pull up to Manning Canning, a preserves company on a small industrial strip in Toronto ringed by the pricey real estate of Leaside. Christine Manning welcomes me in as though it were her home kitchen. "C'mon in!" I have a seat at the counter window as she finishes off a task. Stainless steel work tables gleam, the floors are scrubbed clean and there isn't a drop of jam in sight. In fact, there is no product anywhere. Christine shows off the large mixing tubs, designed like convection ovens to spread the heat evenly around boiling fruit so nothing burns on the bottom. They look like they've never been used. She gives me a primer on the combi, a steamy alternative to the immersive hot water bath. It looks like a large upright bake oven with rows of racks to hold filled jars as they undergo the last step of processing. Everything has to be pristine.

Christine plunks down on a counter stool and tells me about the preserving classes she runs. Breaking down the fear factor is a big part of the work, even for experienced jammers. "People are very intimidated by it. They are afraid to give their friends and family botulism. They don't understand the science behind what makes it safe inside of the jar."

Christine started canning as an adult by doing what

she'd learned watching her mom and nonna. She'd been working as a digital marketer and had a large garden in her own backyard in Scarborough. With too much for her and her husband to eat fresh, she went back to canning big time. In fact, she calls it a bit of an addiction. Even over four seasons, the output was beyond their capacity to consume. Friends who had benefitted from her preserved peaches and spicy tomato jam encouraged her to set up a business. She needed a commercial kitchen and a lot of science. When you are creating new recipes, you have to know about pH levels. The higher the pH, the lower the acid. The lower the acidity, the greater the risk of botulism, so you have to take extra precautions in processing. Using an existing tested recipe is fine for most of us (if you're pulling something from the Internet, be sure the site is reliable). But if you want to experiment with ingredients and flavours, you need to do some research on the science of preserving produce with different levels of acidity. And as research continues, the most effective procedures change.

A method from your grandmother's kitchen may no longer be the way to go. Christine runs a hand across the counter. "There are a lot of things that my nonna did that are no longer considered safe practice."

Sterilizing and processing filled jars in the oven is out. It doesn't guarantee the contents are hot enough throughout to kill off botulism spores. We use meat thermometers for the same reason — to ensure the middle of the turkey has reached the right temperature. There is also a risk of glass cracking in the dry heat. Sealing jars with paraffin wax is another old method that's also unreliable. The seals aren't guaranteed and too often result in spoiled jams. The techniques are disappearing from recipe books because they are no longer considered safe. I'm rethinking my reliance on a few vintage books I've used for a lot of years. And I'm wondering if I'm not as food literate as I thought. Mason jar producer Bernardin's step-by-step instructions call for use of a boiling water canner on both ends.

Bernardin has been making jars and all of the accessories and tools that go with canning for about a hundred years. The jars are the iconic symbol, named for John Landis Mason, who invented the moulded glass bottles with a screw thread at the opening to accommodate a metal ring and sealing cap. I contact Bernardin's executive chef Emery Brine, an appropriate name for a man who makes pickles, among other preserved products. Emery sees the resurgence in preserving. Sales over the last decade or so have gone up by 5 to 8 percent per year, he says. Who hasn't been offered a cocktail or glass of wine in a mason jar lately? Surely it's a style surge. Emery sets me straight. The increase is across all lines, including canning pots, tongs, sieves and labels. And he's become more popular as a guest speaker. He does about one hundred canning demonstrations across Canada each year. That's an increase of 90 percent from six years ago. Just as Getty Stewart has seen in Manitoba, participants want to do it right without poisoning anyone and to know whether their grandparents' methods are still sound — warning: they're usually not.

A few months earlier at a reunion of friends in Kitchener, I convinced our host, Carol Balsillie, to take us on a tour of her root cellar. Balsillie is a holistic nutritionist. Among the other services she offers through her company Wildberry, she teaches new parents how to make baby food. She's had to convince more than one client that it's OK to feed a baby food that hasn't come out of a Heinz pouch. Still, that parents are interested in knowing more is encouraging. Four of us from across Southern Ontario head down the stairs, past the washer and dryer, sports bags and hanging laundry. The cellar is actually a crawlspace with little insulation at the side of the house. It does the trick. Shiny jars of salsa and peaches stand neatly on wooden shelves. We talk about processing all that fruit, and the subject turns to science. Carol researches every step to understand each detail of why preserving works and what's happening along the way. She brings up pH balances and temperature changes. The farmer in our group takes it all in, then throws her hands up with a laugh. "The Mennonites in my town don't worry about any of that stuff."

Perhaps not, but only because they've stuck with recipes that have already been proven to work and work safely today. It would be worth a review, but then that's throwing up another barrier between tree and table.

While Mojgan Fay and others parse out the meaning of a recipe, eight people, including Christine, are sequestered in a back room with thirty jars of jam, marmalade and jelly and a few pastries. They are judges for the marmalade competition, a hotly contested affair that this year drew challengers from across the country and hopefuls including city councillor Mike Layton, son of former NDP leader Jack Layton. It's serious business. This is the next level of literacy, appreciating the best-crafted products, taking time to perfect a recipe and tasting every element.

Christine has a coveted first-place ribbon from the Royal Winter Fair, and she earned a bronze at the World Marmalade Awards. More than 2,500 entrants peel, slice, sugar and strain their way into the competition held at Delmain Mansion and Gardens in Cumbria, UK. Paddington Bear, known lover of marmalade, is a patron, the judges wear white lab coats and a shuttle bus runs among three venues. As a measure of the event's popularity, almost half a million dollars from entry fees has gone to charity. Winning is considered a "marketing gift" that comes with gold roundel stickers to add to jars. It's like slapping a Man Booker logo to the cover of a book, sure to enhance sales.

At Fort York, the judges are looking for a nice aroma with no high bitter or burnt smell. Marmalade must also have a good texture, neither too hard nor too runny. Overcooked marmalade becomes gelatinous and tough to get a spoon into. The peel must be tender and of course the flavour should be nice and orange. Too much cooking and the sugar will burn and caramelize.

The Judges' Choice award will go to Genevieve Shave for a Scotch marmalade made from her great-grandmother's recipe. The whisky's only purpose in the ancestral home was to flavour the preserves.

Marmalade is Christine's favourite preserve to make, not because of the taste, which she does enjoy, but because of the process. It takes time. You can't rush through it and you use every part of the orange. The pith and the seeds add to the pectin, the skin is peeled and sliced, the juice adds to the flavour. Each piece takes another step. "You have to really be present in the process, and I think there is something that comes out of that. It's really rewarding."

That mental reward can't be ignored. It comes from taking a moment to consider the food before you, where it grew and how many hands it has been through. Christine works with two women in her shop and encourages novice canners to do the same, work with friends. "It feels almost like a community activity. You tell stories while you're doing it. We laugh a lot. It's just a really lovely way to prepare food."

LIME CILANTRO MARMALADE

As owner of Manning Canning, Christine Manning is one of the professional entrants in preserving contests close to home and abroad. This recipe created by Christine earned a second-place ribbon at Mad for Marmalade.

Yields approximately six 250 ml jars.

INGREDIENTS

1 cup lime peel zest

2 cups water

¼ cup fresh lime juice (strained)

2½ cups lime segments

½ cup fresh lime juice

5 cups sugar

3 oz liquid pectin

2 tbsp finely chopped cilantro

INSTRUCTIONS

1. *Combine in a bowl the 1 cup of lime zest with 1 cup of water and stir to cover zest completely. Soak for 10–15 minutes, drain and discard the water.*

2. *In a medium-sized pan, combine the peel with the strained lime juice and add remaining cup of water. Using medium-high heat, bring to*

a boil. Reduce the heat once a boil has been achieved, cover and simmer for 10 minutes. Stir in the lime segments and lime juice. Cover and continue to simmer for an additional 10 minutes.

3. Remove the cover, stir in the sugar and continue to stir until the sugar is completely dissolved.

4. Return the heat to medium-high, and stirring constantly, bring the contents to a full rolling boil. Stir in the 3 oz of liquid pectin and return to a rolling boil, stirring constantly. Boil for 1 minute. Remove your pan from the heat and skim off any foam.

5. Quickly stir in the cilantro and allow the marmalade to cool for 5 minutes, stirring occasionally.

6. Ladle your marmalade into previously sterilized jars, leaving a ¼ inch headspace. Wipe the rims and threads and apply lids and screw rings. Process in a 200°F water bath for 10 minutes.

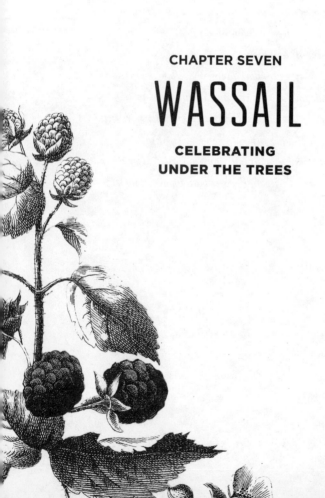

CHAPTER SEVEN

WASSAIL

CELEBRATING
UNDER THE TREES

Bohemian waxwings in cold climates are said to get drunk on winter berries. Whitehorse residents have rescued the wobbly birds from wonky flight paths and window crashes, incarcerating them in hamster-cage drunk tanks until they sober up. Mountain ash and other ornamental berries stick to the trees' branches long after all the leaves have dropped. In a freeze-and-thaw cycle through the fall, the fruit ferments. The little creatures either can't tell the difference or they like the experience. They sip from the juices left in the puckered sacks and gobble down the seeds deep inside. Ice wine for the birds. For the rest of us, it's the end of the season and a return to cold storage apples, frozen berries and preserved peaches and plums.

What if the consumption of fermented berries were a deliberate act on the part of the birds, their own version of a wassail, a drunken celebration under the apple trees? The tradition is believed to have started in Britain around the year 600 to celebrate the harvest, ward off bad luck, ensure a good crop the following season and, it seems, to gather among the trees for good cheer. From the Anglo-Saxon "*waes hael*," the word means "be well." Urban versions of the practice were a precursor to carolling as revellers travelled from house to house with a pewter or silver bowl sloshing full of boozy juice. There's such a bowl at Oxford University's Jesus College that can hold 10 gallons of the warm concoction of spicy cider.

The ritual has some requirements. A head reveller dips a piece of toast, then places the sodden bread in the branches of the biggest or most fruitful tree in the orchard. The toast will feed the robins, believed to be the guardians of the tree. The celebrants gently bend a few boughs to dip them in the bowl too. The whole thing is accompanied by noise from horns and banging pots and buckets, much like the Scottish Hogmanay or New Year's noisemakers or the Lunar New Year firecrackers to wake the tree spirits and drive away evil demons. And with 10 gallons of cider to share, there is singing. Historian and archeologist Kath Bates, writing for Oxford Open Learning, offers this snippet from a traditional song by wassailers:

> *Apple tree, apple tree we all come to wassail thee,*
> *Bear this year and next year to bloom and blow,*
> *Hat fulls, cap fulls, three cornered sacks fills . . .*

It's a hopeful celebration, knowing there is more to come, having faith in the magic underneath the snow on snow on snow. It's a symbolic acknowledgement of our responsibility for the earth, of our willingness to take care of the natural world. It's also a gathering of community, finding another reason off-season to connect under the trees, to say we'll do this again.

More than one thousand people come together each September for Not Far From The Tree's City Cider

Festival, held at Spadina House, the former home of the Austin family, now a Toronto museum and the site of Laura Reinsborough's first pick of fruit from what had been a mostly unused heritage urban orchard.

Like Isaac Newton and Eve and their apples, a lot developed from Laura's first pull from a tree. The heritage gardener on staff, Wendy Woodworth, admits it was kind of neat to be there when Laura discovered that pleasure. "This is a very nice piece of property. The orchard has a nice vibe about it. It's a very comfortable kind of place." So better for Laura to be here than in a commercial orchard full of machines. "It was just this lovely kind of rural experience within a city area."

That pick set off a chain of events that put the orchard to a different use. The museum had an active kitchen program at one time and used a lot of the fruit to make cookies, cakes, sauces and jellies to share with visitors, but in recent years, that had stopped.

Before Not Far From The Tree made this a destination pick, Wendy would take bags of apples to the Riverdale Farm, another city-owned property, to feed to the horses and cows. The animals were happy to have them, but the apples were a harder sell to humans. Many of the old varieties have fallen out of favour because they don't keep well, so most landed in the compost heap. Now here we are today, delighted to be guzzling down cider, hard and soft, squished out of those same trees, some of it pressed just moments ago. With a large crowd, the apples were supplemented with crops from picks elsewhere in the city, including some I'd had my own hands on. Another postage-stamp yard behind a rented semidetached house had been farmed to the hilt at one time. Left over was a nasty-looking apple tree, a fabulous yellow plum and a healthy patch of raspberry canes. The apples were rock-hard bitter, but they've added something to the blend we're drinking now. It's a brilliant lesson from the boughs. Look up, they say. Use what you have.

A gaggle of kids is at work, helping to wash and chop bushels of apples. Others are swarmed by wasps as they process hundreds of pounds of fruit through a wooden press, the liquid slowly trickling into a pot, then sieve and boil (just in case) the juice into a hot nectar.

A couple of dozen trees stand on the north side of the six-acre grounds. Some are well over one hundred years old and they still fruit. I can see, especially in the upper branches, far beyond reach of any pick poles I've used, classic red apples against grey sky. Some, not so tall, look like they've seen better days. One is so hollowed out, the trunk looks like a turkey carcass, full of skeletal angles jutting into a dark maw. As an amateur, I'd think it was finished, at risk of falling, but it too has fruit on the branches. Grapevines on wire fencing ring the orchard. A worker's cottage sits just beyond. It used to house the family's driver. Now it's full of equipment and its bedrooms turned into overstuffed offices. On the roadside to the west is a large greenhouse.

Four generations of the Austin family lived here, starting with James Austin in 1866, building a well-to-do life from railways, banking and gas. I imagine the Austins spent time at the edge of the property, admiring the view overlooking Lake Ontario in the distance. The family gathered there to watch fireworks marking the historic events of July 1, 1867, the country's first Dominion Day. The apples would have been just forming into green bulbs at the time.

Thirty varieties of apples still grow here, varieties you won't find in stores: maiden's blush, red astrachan and snow apples. Because we don't recognize them, and even when we do, Wendy sees the doubt many visitors have about whether the fruit is edible. It is. The apples may not be pretty; because it's a city property, they don't spray the fruit. Wendy picks up an apple from the ground, runs a thumb over a brown patch on the skin. "That's apple scab. You can cut around it," she says, and there are other things that mar the fruit. "This one doesn't appear to have a worm in it, but sometimes they do." Insects lay eggs when the fruit still has a flower, so the worm grows inside the apple. "It's pretty clean. They're vegetarian worms that have never touched the ground," she laughs. "They're not going to hurt you either."

Austin and many like him made horticultural societies part of their social lives. It was an activity of gentlemen. "They had full-time jobs, but they spent a lot of time and energy being involved in a hort society and growing their prize chrysanthemums or whatever else it was and going to meetings. They were fairly scientific about the whole thing."

Wendy puzzles over why that stopped. Perhaps we've reached information overload. "Maybe there was less information around and so it was easier to focus on things and be interested in particular subjects and know as much as there was to know."

We credit technology for creating a means to find all of that information and source it from anywhere in the world. But we also blame it for giving us the leisure activities that keep us inside on screens more than ever. "It was social to go out to meetings, to be involved in a society and go to lectures," Wendy says, and it was an exciting time in the plant world. "It was early enough in the [European] history of Canada that people were still trying to find out what was possible here."

Hints of that social life through plants are returning, and to those who are involved, some of that same excitement. Seedy Saturdays held across the country in more than 110 locations are their own celebration of plant life, including an opportunity to swap seeds, talk to other gardeners about the provenance of seeds, take in a workshop, listen to a lecture and find out what grows best in a very local climate. Plant swaps and shares do the same, offering gardeners plants from others like them who know the peculiarities, likes and dislikes of the plant in question.

The kitchen help would have used Austin's carefully

curated orchard and garden produce for meals and entertaining. The family followed menus and recipes from its Northern Irish heritage, so many of the plants would have been sourced from Britain. Not all of the apple varieties would grow in the Canadian climate, so Austin had to work at finding something that would. The master of the house also had an intellectual interest in seeing what he could grow here.

As a city farmer today, Wendy has some benefits Austin wouldn't have enjoyed. Growth and development have created city microclimates. Dense and dark concrete, brick buildings and asphalt absorb heat and then release it along with all of the heat that pours out of cars and warmed buildings, creating a heat island. Tall buildings can block wind or create wind tunnels. So a bad winter for farmers might not affect fruit trees in the city. Higher temperatures also open the door to more varieties of fruit. I look at the oldest trees and wonder how they've survived severe weather over the years. Toronto was hit by a hurricane in the '50s, and just a few years back an ice storm wiped out power to large swaths of the region as branches fell under the weight. But these trees survived it all. Wendy credits good pruning and stability. The orchard has been intact for more than a century.

She points to the spot where a delicious apple tree grew, coaxed along over many years. She watched the trunk rot until all that was left was a semicircle with one branch. Even at that, it continued bearing apples for several years until someone kicked it over. Wendy was angry. She wanted it to live on. "It was such a neat thing that it would do that. Plant life is like that. The will to live is extraordinary."

The cider event draws to the grounds far more people than the museum usually sees in a day, if not a week. Guests wander through the trees, check out the orchard and the heritage kitchen garden with its massive rhubarb plants, press apples, listen to music and eat and drink fruit products. Notable chefs serve food made with fruit they've helped pick from city yards. Cider producers offer the fermented juice of apples, pears and cranberries in mason jars. People lounge on the wide wooden veranda, lay blankets on the grass, tap croquet mallets on wooden balls and learn about bees and apples. Joshna Maharaj is one of the chef participants.

Joshna remembers her father planting a cherry tree in the family's Thornhill backyard. Even as a preteen she was interested in food and had big expectations for that tree. Her dad had to explain that it was a much longer-term investment. "Even by the time we had moved out, there were no cherries," she laments. "So frequently when we'd drive by our old house, I'd be like, 'I bet they got those cherries this year.'" She remembers thinking, "Somewhere, somehow, somebody is going to eat those cherries." Those cherries may have evaded her, but the city has offered some consolation bounty: today, her team serves up duck with a serviceberry chutney and a dried serviceberry garnish. They picked the berries themselves, connecting chefs with the bounty of the city.

Farzam Fallah, pastry chef at the farm-to-table restaurant Richmond Station, presents hay-infused ice cream topped with cooked-out apricots he picked from a city backyard. He talks about the dish as though the ingredients are precious gems. I have to remind myself that all food comes from the ground; the fact that these apricots hail from a Toronto laneway doesn't make them any less valuable.

Alexandra Feswick, the chef de cuisine at the Drake Hotel, battles the swarms of wasps to offer sticky candied crabapples. The crabapples weren't her first choice; she's not alone in that, but figured she'd never cooked with them before, so why not. It's a bit like the television food competitions where the contestants are handed a basket of improbable ingredients, then judged on the results. She could have gone with the default jelly but took on the responsibility that comes with wearing the chef's whites. "If you can take a common ingredient and teach someone something different that you can do with that, then I think that's an important part of our jobs as chefs."

Her team pickled the sour, mealy apples overnight with white vinegar, apple juice, oranges, cinnamon, star anise and a lot of sugar. They poured the hot mixture onto the apples and let them steam in the liquid. The next day they threaded them on skewers, dipped them in caramel sauce and rolled them in pecans. I pop one in my mouth quickly, swatting away the wasps. It's a lovely, messy treat.

A few days later, my kids are appalled when I head down the street with a stepladder to pick crabapples from a neighbour's tree. When I ask if she'd mind, the neighbour tells me I'd be doing her a favour. She's asked the city to prune the beast to stop the branches from catching hats and hair of passersby. I come home with two large bags and spend an afternoon stewing half into applesauce. It took a lot of sugar to stop the mouth puckering, and I needed a better sieve to remove the seeds and cores. I used some of the sauce to bake into cookies and sent a batch over to the neighbour. She seemed surprised at the result, even though she does eat the odd fruit from the tree. We added the rest to yogurt throughout the week. The second bag went into jars with spiced vinegar, again with a lot of sugar. That recipe came from the Bernardin website.

The crabapples are always a hard sell even for a harvest organization with massive wait lists. The celebrity pick with Alexandra didn't fill up. Alexandra is realistic about the average person's capacity for cooking. She knows her recipe was a bit labour intensive. But there are very simple ways to use crabapples. "You can put them in a slow cooker with some sugar and they'll make themselves. There's really actually no labour required if you're doing that."

Professional chef or not, she says the effort is always worth it. "I believe in cooking locally as much as possible just because I simply think that an apple tastes better picked from a tree as opposed to sitting on the truck. So if we can do something with them, then why wouldn't we?"

Joshna is of the same mind. Seeing a source of food in city trees, rather than assuming that everything is poisonous, makes things friendlier, she says. "This poisonous berry dismissal really puts you oppositionally to your community. This notion that the life that grows is poisonous is a problem." It's evidence of our gross disconnection with nature and food. "We are so far away that we don't imagine that something growing naturally would be full of sweet delicious things."

I take that notion and put it to the test. I often walk through Mount Pleasant Cemetery in midtown Toronto. It takes me off busy Yonge Street and under the trees. Later in the fall, I notice a terrible odour and wonder if there is trouble among the graves. It's a pair of ginkgo trees, shedding fruit with the telltale stink of illness and rot. I track down a groundskeeper and ask him about this odd choice for a cemetery. He tells me most of the trees are planted not by the administration, but by request of loved ones. So the family of this soul buried by the tree must have felt she had a special connection with the fan-shaped-leaf trees. They are lovely until they fruit.

In his early days on the job, the groundskeeper remembers seeing crowds of people foraging around the tree. Rather than shoo them away, he roped off the area and gave them boundaries so they could carry off as much of the fetid fruit as they wished. A delicacy in some parts of Asia, the nut of the maidenhair, as it's also known, is said to have health benefits. But, raw, it is toxic. Eating too many, even cooked, can cause vomiting, pains, spasms and breathing difficulties.

I cone my newspaper into a container, drop in a dozen ginkgoes and head home to see what the fuss is about. I've already misstepped. You should wear protective gloves when handling the fruit to avoid the toxins. Golden orbs of fruit look very tempting, but I know enough not to pierce the skin until I'm ready for the smell. Following a YouTube tutorial, I put them into a bowl of water outside for a few hours to soften the fruit. Then, gloved this time, I pop the nuts out of the pulp and scrub off the flesh. Once they've dried on a cookie sheet, I slip them into the oven to roast until they've begun to split open. An alien-like almost fluorescent green glows through the shell, one of those colours that never looks natural. Mindful of the toxicity warnings, I crack one open and take a delicate bite, telling my daughters what I'm doing, just in case. Chestnutty, but milder, it tastes nothing like the fruit smells. I offer a nut to our family gathered for Thanksgiving. There are no takers. To Joshna's point, it does change my idea of what's hanging in the trees of the city. Rather than dismissing the stink fruit, I looked to the wider community, studied up and found a way to connect. The trepidation around ginkgoes is a wise one. Apples on the other hand are only poisonous in fairy tales, and even then you need the intervention of an evil queen to make them so.

The wassail in whatever form it takes is as much a celebration of what we do with the fruit as it is of the trees. Interest in food and plants is showing a hopeful turn. The Canadian-based not-for-profit Culinary Tourism Alliance started up in 2006, meeting an interest in travel based on food. The United Nations World Tourism Association held its first international forum on food tourism in 2015. Food workshops are increasingly popular and so is canning.

A salsa band has started playing; pockets of dancing break out — couples who know what they're doing, kids who spin uninhibited and others who move to the beat, a little skip in their steps, cider spilling over the sides of their jars.

I imagine the Austins picking fruit or having cider from these trees and the pleasure their descendants might get from eating from the same tree today, tasting what their great-great-grandfather did. Although they visit the house privately from time to time, no one at the museum could recall seeing them picking in the orchard. Still, I like to think that Austin would be pleased to see a celebration among his trees once more.

SERVICEBERRY CHUTNEY

Rossy Earle created this recipe from berries picked on campus at Ryerson University. Rossy and Joshna Maharaj, working with Ryerson Eats, served the chutney at City Cider.

Rossy is chef and owner of Supicucu Diablo's Fuego Hot Sauce. She grew up in Panama and had no idea there were so many fruit trees on campus. She'd never worked with serviceberries and was excited to create something with fruit picked on site. She finds the berries to be very versatile.

INGREDIENTS

2 cups serviceberries

2 garlic cloves, minced

1 cup red onion, finely diced

2 tbsp fresh ginger root, minced

1 cup brown sugar, packed

½ cup honey

½ cup white wine

¼ cup apple cider vinegar

1 tbsp fresh lemon juice

1 tsp lemon zest

Pinch kosher salt

Cracked black pepper

1 tbsp fresh parsley, chopped

1 tbsp fresh thyme, chopped

2 scallions, chopped

INSTRUCTIONS

1. *Combine all ingredients, except scallions, parsley and thyme, in a saucepan.*
2. *Bring to a boil over medium heat, stirring frequently.*
3. *Cook for 8–10 minutes until the mixture is the consistency of jam. Add scallions and herbs during the last 2 minutes of cooking.*
4. *Remove from heat and cool completely.*

Chutney will keep in the fridge for about a month.

CONCLUSION

WAITING FOR SPRING

Our backyard looks bedraggled. The spectacle of fall has passed, the promise of spring is months off; plant tags stick out of the soil like gravestones. I run a quick inventory of the fruit bushes I've planted over the years: two currant berries that disappeared after two seasons; raspberries that have spread into the gardens and lawn but don't yield enough for a cereal bowl; a serviceberry — "it needs no care at all," said the clerk in the nursery — that gave us one season of fruit; a rhubarb plant that needs more sun than we can offer; and an elderberry we picked up at a native species plant sale (some creature snapped it off in August; the boots of a utility crew installing new wires finished the job in January). Our only reliable source of fruit is the invasive mulberry tree. Without pruning or water, it has grown to the rooftop, extending its branches 12 feet from the trunk. I have a freezer full of containers packed with the purple nodes just from the few branches that reach over our flat roof. The squirrels, raccoons and birds have eaten the rest.

Fruit pickers and growers across the country have convinced me to reconsider the borders of my garden, to look at the shared resources beyond our city lot. So when our church made plans to create a mini orchard on the lawn last spring, I signed up to help. The property gets plenty of sun on a corner lot at the top of a hill. The Gothic-style building opened in 1917. Congregations over the years have added stained glass windows, a pipe organ and solar panels. Otherwise, the basic structure has remained the same: grey stone with a two-storey bell tower, the sanctuary and fellowship hall attached in an L-shape configuration. Tucked into the middle space is a square lawn that in my memory had no trees at all on it until a spruce was added in the 2000s. Members installed a community vegetable garden a few years ago, and then with grant support, they were offered free trees and a coaching package from Susan Poizner.

I put my boot on the spade and push until I hear the crunch of splitting roots. The yard is well tamped from neighbours walking dogs, kids taking breaks from summer camps and the occasional picnic or barbecue. I use my full body weight, both feet on the spade, bouncing to push farther into the dark dirt below. Hole achieved, we toss in a shovelful of compost made from the food garden scraps, drop in the tree, put back the soil and tamp it down. Nature quickly takes care of the watering. The minister says a prayer of thanks and we move on to seeding the beds.

The responsibility of nature stewardship runs across many cultures and religions. In some Orthodox Jewish traditions, it is considered wrong to cut down a fruit tree. The Bible says even in war, let them grow. "Thou shalt not destroy the trees thereof by wielding an axe against them; for thou mayest eat of them, but thou shalt not cut them down; for is the tree of the field man, that it should be besieged of thee?"

In other words, leave the fruit trees alone. They aren't people, you have no quarrel with them and you can eat from them. Others in the Jewish community believe the consequences of ignoring those words could be dire.

The warning was well heeded by the owners of Shloimy's Bake Shoppe on 12th Avenue in Brooklyn. They had plans to expand their shop a few years back, but when they discovered a fruit tree in the way, they had to change the designs, building a glass enclosure open to the sky to house the plant. Another family in the Midwood neighbourhood of Brooklyn had put up with an unwanted mulberry tree that had been loathed by neighbours because of its messy droppings on sidewalks and cars. As observant Jews, they couldn't take the tree down. The *Brooklyn Daily* reported that an act of God fixed that for them. Hurricane Irene took out the tree in 2011. As for the wrath of God, the power was out for 20 hours, a car was totalled and a piece of the owner's foundation was damaged.

The church trees did well that first season. The organizers chose pears and apples. If they can keep them safe from flying Frisbees, errant cartwheels and peeing dogs, they should see fruit in a few years. And in an organization built on tradition, the trees could still be feeding neighbours in one hundred years' time. That's the plan. It's for the neighbourhood and it's for who comes later.

Lee Herrin and Matt Strand were doing the same thing: planting an idea that would bear fruit for years to come. They made a portable concept that's been used these decades later across the continent. The largest in Canada is Not Far From The Tree. It's grown from 150 volunteers harvesting 3,000 pounds of fruit in 2008 to 1,800 volunteers picking tens of thousands of pounds of fruit from 1,800 registered trees.

Laura Reinsborough moved to Toronto for environmental studies at York University and graduated from the same master's program as Lee Herrin. Two people from opposite sides of the country study at the same institution a decade apart and, within a year of graduating, each creates a new organization devoted to picking city fruit. That's pretty remarkable. The university can't explain the connection.

The Green Living Show is coming up at the city's convention centre, and Laura will be speaking on a panel about food waste. Examining and dealing with waste as it affects everything from hunger to garbage is gaining steam on food security agendas. It's been among the motivators for urban harvesters across Canada. I've spoken to a half a dozen of them, looking for trends, similarities and what sparked them to get started in the trees. So when I ask a presumptive question of Laura about using wasted fruit as a starting point, I'm surprised at the answer: "It doesn't break my heart to see it fall to the ground."

"Maybe it's like, don't cry over spilled milk," she says, adding that it's not that food isn't important, but that she sees it as a tool in community engagement around environmental issues, building community, a stronger sense of safety and belonging within a city, and "more connection with the soil underneath your feet."

I get what Laura's saying, but then she adds, "I really struggle with defining this as a food security project." And I'm caught off guard. Picking existing free food and sharing it with people who don't have enough and particularly not enough fresh food sounds like a food security venture to me. It works to ensure everyone has access to safe, nutritious and appropriate food.

Laura continues, careful to couch her language with personal perspectives; there is no pontificating when she says, "To me, food security is not an end goal." Rather, the goal has more to do with social justice, environmental connection, access, equity and environmental sustainability.

"The waste is part of it," Laura says, "but I think that the reason we're using this existing source of fruit is to get to something even more than that. That's why I do it."

I've seen how the act of coming together to pick fruit does engage us. It's a bit like a barn raising or quilting bee, only we often don't know who it's in aid of. I tell her about the stories I've heard in the trees. About the luck it takes to score a spot on a pick and why people are so keen to participate. I remember a conversation in the branches of a yellow plum tree in a group where everyone was a teacher of one kind or another — music, college, high school. We talked about why we were there. The college environmental studies professor said she wanted to stay connected to local environmental programs, to keep her hand in the field. A retired teacher enjoyed the activity of picking. A young man, newly graduated from university and just starting his career, was straight up about his interest. "I'm just here for the fruit. That's it." He was ready to take his share and anything left over.

In the harvesters' office, green painter's tape and sticky notes are pressed onto the wall, left over from a board meeting as members worked to lay out the organization's updated mission and goals. Because Laura is on a grant proposal deadline, I expect she's thought hard about articulating a definition, but she says the board has struggled about how much to define. "It's a very powerful message to keep open," she takes, focusing on the wall notes. "If we just talk about *what* we do, people find their own meaning from it." To illustrate, she recounts what happens when she gives her elevator pitch, the short, crisp door opener she uses when she meets a prospective partner or funder. "People cut me off before I get to the why of what we do," she says, getting really animated acting out the parts. "'We pick fruit from trees in the city . . .' 'Oh! That's a brilliant idea, there's a tree around the corner and I always thought what a waste,' 'We grew up picking and I know how many pies you could make from that' and 'You give it to food banks and shelters. That's incredible. They need access.' People find their own meaning from it, so we don't want to dictate what that meaning is. But for me, the meaning is multiple and it's hard to contribute just to one."

I think about what I've taken from the city harvest concept and try to determine what it means to me. First,

I like the access to fruit grown in my own city. Picking it myself, as Laura found, is fun. It's going outside with a purpose. I enjoy meeting new people and talking to strangers. We become part of a team and part of a network that does something significant with a backyard tree. Making a meal or dessert with fruit I picked from a house down the road lets me make the farm-to-table connection even clearer for my daughters. Over time, I started thinking more about how old some of the trees are. When the homeowners are around, we can find out a bit of the provenance of the trees, how many families have lived in arm's reach of a cherry, for example. The stories usually start with an old guy from the old country. Even though that "old guy" may have been working in manual labour all day, he had the energy to coddle his trees when he got home in a way that few of us feel we can today. And then there are the positive feelings that come from helping get fruit to someone who wouldn't otherwise have access to it. A helper's high is not insignificant. Doing "good" improves emotional well-being and self-worth, which help with overall mental health.

I ask Laura to give me the end of her elevator pitch, the part that tells me what it all means to her. The end of the pitch should be limited to one sentence, but I suspect it's not going to go that way with her. "For me," she says, "it's about connecting with urban ecology and even just recognizing the city as an ecological space, and then about making good use of local food." She laughs. "That is like a gateway drug. If you can better tap into the rhythms of seasonality, then you can seek out more local food in your diet from other sources." She finishes her end-of-pitch statement with access. "[We want] to make sure that that's not just for those who can afford it at farmers' markets."

I'm glad she's brought that up. For a variety of reasons, local produce often costs more than imported. I think of the always-on-sale California strawberries as an example. So farmers' markets, while lovely, may be beyond some budgets. With patience, in theory, anyone can access a city orchard harvest for free. Laura wraps up the pitch, which consists of "the health and nutrition, access and equity piece. So, yeah, it's still everything."

When Lee started, he dreamed of running the organization free of grants and government support, making it self-sustaining. I put the question to Laura. With free fruit and free labour, is it possible to do this in a self-sustaining way without the support of grants?

Laura furrows her brows at the question. I can see "no" in her eyes, but she's prepared to give a full response. "I find it difficult to see that happening without there being strain and sacrifice on the other resources that are involved." She moves on to what she acknowledges is a flawed premise. But it's a good illustration. "On a commercial orchard, it's often one landowner, one property owner and there's a lot more control over what is happening," she starts. I think of Chudleigh's Farm in Milton, Ontario, which we visited in the fall, and the Cherry Avenue Farms in Lincoln, Ontario, where we gorged on peaches and nectarines. There is a lot of family involved in the upkeep of these farms, perhaps there also for the love of it. And then there were the many orchards we've passed on the highway and beyond. Not as large and perhaps not as prosperous. "It's still a huge struggle to make it all break even," Laura says, "and though our give and take of resources is different from a commercial orchard, we have 1,300 property owners on our land with 1,600 trees. We're not likely to find a comparable example of a commercial orchard. As I say, there are huge holes in this comparison," she continues, pointing out the logistics of asking permission and coordinating with all the tree owners. "There's the free resource of the volunteers, but the training and support and recognition and the tools that are needed to organize those logistics, well, those add up." The organization harvested from about 350 trees in her last year at the helm in about 260 separate picking events. "That's organizing 260 events!"

Lee's hopes for a bigger entrepreneurial spirit and his desire to see urban harvesters use commercial tools to promote their social aims haven't taken hold.

The preserve-selling Fruitful was a mini social enterprise for Not Far From The Tree one year, but Laura says it was an additional load of work. "There are ways that we could integrate it more seamlessly, but it's not generated revenue from what we're already doing." That means finding someone to take it on as a full-time unpaid job, "and burn themselves out," she adds.

For a city-based harvest outfit, Laura is skeptical of

the benefits of the large-scale social enterprise sustaining the core activity. "I think there are revenue streams available for this work and I'm supportive of that. We're considering what that could look like for us. But in the end, like for most nonprofits and charities, earned income would total 10–15 percent. It's hard to think of a social enterprise really covering its own costs in addition to covering the program and operation costs."

Hidden Harvest has come close, raising almost 70 percent of its small operating budget by running family-friendly midway games for a local brewery's Octoberfest celebration. The event has nothing to do with picking fruit, but takes advantage of the loyal Hidden Harvest volunteers who show up to do the work for free.

I started this tour looking for things I could quantify — all the how many's and percentages that could fit on spreadsheets. The number of trees, the volume of fruit, the volunteers recruited, dollars granted, waste averted and people fed. Access to big data has led us to want more information, even though we have more than ever. It's a time of abundance in a different form. Because the numbers are available, we want to have them, and having them may give them more significance than they warrant.

If you parsed out the value of an individual tree — the cost in time to plant, prune, pick and preserve each year might well exceed the retail value of the yield if you chose to source it at a discount grocery store.

But then I think about Francesco and his fig tree,

making something grow because you can, because you figured out how to conquer the New World. The new owners of that fig are debating whether to keep it, but a woman I met at the Mad for Marmalade celebration had no such hesitation. Mya Sangster is a stalwart of the Culinary Historians of Canada, a retired teacher and a maker of marmalade. Unlike most of the entrants at the marmalade competitions, Mya grows her own oranges in midtown Toronto. Many florists sell miniature indoor citrus fruits, so I was curious to see how many plants she'd have to give her a batch of preserves.

In late winter, she walked me through her house to the back door in the kitchen, stopping to put on a red parka and bundling up a cereal box for the recycling bin. The snow had picked up, and I felt bad for taking her outside on a last-minute visit. She waved off my concern and pointed out the bare apple and pear trees in the backyard. There had been peach trees too, but they caught a disease. The Portuguese have a saying: he who wants to leave nothing to his heirs plants an orchard of peaches.

We headed the few steps to a greenhouse, cloudy glass panes above a brick-and-wood foundation. Mya swung open the door, unveiling a massive orange tree. It took up almost the entire space, pushing at the ceiling, hunched over like Alice in Wonderland when she's very big. The scent of orange was sharp, the air moist and warm and the soil beneath our feet soft. Oranges dotted the branches, bright citrus against dark green leaves. It was magnificent.

The house and greenhouse went up in 1948, heated through the same system of hot water radiators. Nine rusty pipes run along the walls, radiating enough heat to keep the space above freezing. Replacing the glass has added to the cost as the thriving tree elbows through a few panes every now and then. Assuming the tree was planted at about the same time as the greenhouse went up, it would be nearly 70 years old. Mya was sure it's a Sicilian orange. The odds are it came directly from Italy.

Mya, her husband and children moved in in the early '80s, buying the property from the original owners, an Italian family. Two generations had lived here, growing fruit in the backyard and selling fruit in a nearby green grocery shop. The history fan and her botanist husband have kept the greenhouse going for another 30 years, taking care of three figs and an orange tree. The figs never did well and were quickly overshadowed by the burgeoning orange.

Some of last year's fruit was still hanging, mixed in with newer specimens and fresh blossoms. Mya had me pull a few fruits off the tree. Her arm was weak from a break she had suffered. She looked at the dusting of white fungus on the skins and sighed. The windows needed cleaning, and there was more work to be done on the tree. "My husband is not well, and there are other things to do in life."

They had someone come in to prune not long before. Mya had no idea what the financial tally had been over the years. It didn't matter. She couldn't let the tree die. She and her husband, long retired, were aging. Her children had no interest in the tree or the greenhouse. She knew what would come next. "Our house is going to be a teardown and that'll go, which saddens me greatly."

Heating a greenhouse year-round for the privilege of growing Seville oranges would go well beyond any accountant's advice for a sound financial decision. It was never about the cost. It was never even about survival for Mya or the family before her. Growing your own fruit, harvesting fruit, is about the connection to nature, understanding the needs of something as basic as a tree. It's about saying, "I did that. I created food where there was none." And it's about the people you meet as a result. I'm not the only curious visitor Mya has met.

We don't have to build a greenhouse or take on the most exotic fruits to be part of these connections. Looking up from the tie-dyed sidewalk and seeing the berries overhead is enough to remind us that food does grow on trees, even in the city, and you can learn a lot by taking a bite.

Soon after our chat, Laura left her enterprise and the city of six million. With her partner, author and musician Chris Eaton, and their two young children, she headed back home to Sackville, New Brunswick, not far from the Bay of Fundy, a university town of 5,500 surrounded by windswept marshes and coastal cliffs.

She had no plans to set up a similar organization in Sackville.

I run through some exit interview questions to see where they take us. I expect she'd be proud of the numbers of trees picked, the growth of the organization or even the waste diverted. She thinks for a moment before saying her pride is in helping other groups. "We're not the first and we're not the last, and whenever somebody calls us for advice, my assumption is that they are also calling a few other similar projects. Wouldn't it be great if there was a 1-800 number you could just call and get it all started . . ."

I think of the downloadable instruction package from LifeCycles and the chart of organizations I've made. It sounds like a potential social enterprise to me, a city harvest start-up consultant service. She tips her head and pushes back a strand of hair from her face. "I know we aren't the only ones contributing advice and support in this, but I feel really honoured any time somebody does reach out and says, 'Hey, we want to do something similar to Not Far From The Tree.'" Those calls have come from across the country and from around the world. "It's been really rewarding to see that, just by answering that call, just by sending an email back that we've played a role in being able to help other groups."

Laura's epiphany while picking that first heritage apple changed her view of the city. As she's getting ready to leave, I discover it's changed her view of the country too. Thinking of the men and women who brought branches overseas to graft on trees here that she's been harvesting, I ask her what she will take on her journey back home. She has to think for a moment. "Nothing physical comes to mind." She pauses again before choosing her words carefully. "I think that what I hope to take with me is a bit of that, hmm, I feel like I'm perpetuating the same divide by saying it this way, but a bit of that urban sensibility, that caring for every patch of land, like something this size," she says as she gestures to the small pale green children's table between us. "There's a cherry tree up on a parking lot on St. Clair growing from a space not much bigger than this, and it can make 12 pies every year."

I'm picturing many similar trees growing in peculiar spaces despite the odds.

"In urban spaces we do a lot with small little snippets of land, and I don't want to lose that, that feeling of possibility."

Just as it was possible for Francesco to grow his fig tree in a cold city lot, and it was possible for people to eat from that tree years after Francesco was gone, the trees make it possible to take the best of what was left and turn it into something of our own. Look up and imagine what can be done. No laws have to be passed, no buildings felled or degrees earned to harness the power of the city fruit tree. It requires attitudinal, not agricultural, changes.

Lee Herrin said it's no big deal to pick your neighbour's fruit and share it. We've made it one by losing the skills, choosing convenience and forgetting about waste in a world of abundance. Maybe it won't always be a big deal. Maybe we'll make it the most natural thing in the world to pick through your neighbour's tree the way you might pick up a book from a box of discards at the curb.

Perhaps there will be a time when we take a break at work and step out to the community orchard for a fresh pear.

I leave Laura to her grant proposal and go in search of a small patch of land by a parking lot with a cherry tree waiting for spring.

ACKNOWLEDGEMENTS

This book was developed with the support of the University of King's College Master of Fine Arts in Creative Nonfiction program. My thanks go to the mentors, visiting authors and editors and to fellow writers who saw the possibility of a book about fruit. In particular, I thank Don Sedgwick, David Swick, Harry Thurston, Tim Falconer and the dazzling Jane Silcott, who, in addition to reading the early chapters, carried a jar of crabapple jelly from one coast to the other to offer me a taste.

My thanks to editor Jen Knoch, who embraced the concept, bringing not only her skill with words and story to the project, but a passion for growing food and the enthusiasm of the ECW team. I thank Jen for seeing the forest beyond my trees.

Many others, friends, acquaintances and colleagues, contributed to this story through sidewalk conversations, notes on fruits, recollections of their family trees and time listening to my ideas. Thank you all. I am also grateful for the resourcefulness of librarians everywhere and to library patrons who watched my stuff while I worked my way through the stacks.

I am most appreciative of the time and advice offered by the many volunteers and staff of urban harvest organizations across the country. While running their organizations on shoestrings, some also working day jobs, they took the time to answer my questions with thought and patience. My thanks to Laura Reinsborough, Sue Arndt and the Not Far From The Tree network of volunteers who didn't mind that I took notes during picks. You are all supreme to me. Thanks also to Shannon Lambie of the Vancouver Fruit Tree Project, Getty Stewart, Katrina Siks, Matthew Kemshaw and Lee Herrin.

In addition to Nat Vaccaro and the Shiell-Cappel family, who allowed me into the life of Francesco's fig tree, I am forever grateful to the many people who open their homes and back gates to allow unknown harvesters to pick from their trees. We are strangers no more.

Most importantly, I am grateful for the support of my family, who offered advice, cheerleading and patience throughout. Thank you to Havard for love and kindness and for seeing the book in my story from the start. I thank Gwendolyn for introducing me to urban harvesting, Nell for tasting everything and joining me in the kitchen, Margaret for enduring endless stops on our wanderings across the city to fill one more container of berries, and Judy, Susan and their families for sharing stories from their travels.

> *"Here's to thee, old apple-tree,*
> *Whence thou mayst bud, and whence thou mayst*
> *blow!*
> *And whence thou mayst bear apples enow!*
> *Hats full! Caps full!*
> *Bushel-bushel-sacks full,*
> *And my pockets full too! Huzza!"*

— TRADITIONAL WASSAIL TOAST

NOTES AND SOURCES

Formal research for this book took place over several years, largely as I worked my way through city streets and backyards on the hunt for fruit trees and as I picked fruit with Not Far From The Tree. I had many conversations in those trees and with home gardeners who'd become experts on their small patches of agriculture. Not all of those conversations have made their way into the book, although many of the overriding themes have.

Almost everyone I've spoken to about this book over the years has had a story to add. It's a reminder that, whether we think so or not, we are all touched by urban fruit trees.

Informally, my research has taken place throughout my life, from my first childhood taste of a warm peach pulled from our own backyard tree to helping my dad with the planting and weeding to digging into the dirt in our own city yard.

Books on the themes of fruit, food and food security have inspired my writing and informed my research. Among them are Michael Pollan's *The Omnivore's Dilemma*; David Mas Masimoto's *Epitaph for a Peach*; *The Edible City*, edited by Christina Palassio and Alana Wilcox; Lorraine Johnson's *City Farmer*; Eva Selhub and Alan Logan's *Your Brain on Nature*; Sarah Elton's *Consumed*; Ava Chin's *Eating Wildly*; Adam Leith Gollner's *The Fruit Hunters*; Nick Saul and Andrea Curtis's *The Stop*; and Dorothy Duncan's *Canadians at Table*.

I've included chapter-by-chapter references here in the order that the information appears in the text.

INTRODUCTION. FRANCESCO'S FIG

"Food Loss and Food Waste." Food and Agriculture Organization of the United Nations, Accessed July 17, 2017.

Gooch, M., B. Dent, A.S. Felfel, L. Vanclief, and P. Whitehead. *Food Waste: Aligning Government and Industry Within Value Chain Solutions*. Edited by S. Caroline Glasbey. Value Chain Management International. October 4, 2016.

Canadian Food Inspection Agency. "Local Food Claims
Interim Policy." Government of Canada. September
23, 2014.

"Food for Thought: How Canadians' Dietary Choices
Are Influencing Food Purchases." Nielson.com.

"Farmers Markets and Direct-to-Consumer Marketing."
AMS.usda.gov.

1 • PUTTING DOWN ROOTS. IMMIGRANTS
ARRIVE BEARING FRUIT

Koç, Mustafa, and Jennifer Welsh. "Food, Foodways
and Immigrant Experience." Paper written for the
Multiculturalism Program, Department of Canadian
Heritage at the Canadian Ethnic Studies Association
Conference, November 2001, Halifax.

Doyle, Sabrina. "Canada's Long History of Apple
Growing." *Canadian Geographic*, August 12, 2016.

"Daily Life: Foodways." HistoryMuseum.ca.

Champlain, Samuel de. *Voyages of Samuel de Champlain*.
Translated by Charles Pomeroy Otis. Early
Canadiana Online, 1880.

Carte particulière du Fleuve Saint Louis dressée sur
les lieux avec les noms des sauvages du païs, des
marchandises qu'on y porte & qu'on en reçoit & des
animaux, insectes, poissons, oiseaux, arbres & fruits
des parties septentrionales et méridionales de ce
païs. Archives of Ontario. Archives of Ontario map
collection, C 279-0-0-0-10, reference code AO 2419.

Bénéteau, Marcel. "Jesuit Pear Trees." In *Encyclopédie du patrimoine culturel de l'Amérique française — histoire, culture, religion, héritage*. Article published December 15, 2008.

Parks Plan 2013–2017. City of Toronto Parks, Forestry and Recreation Division website.

Bobiwish, Rodney, and Heather Howard. "Toronto's Native History." *FNH Magazine*, December 4, 2012.

Robertson, Ross J. *The Diary of Mrs. John Graves Simcoe, Wife of the First Lieutenant-Governor of the Province of Upper Canada, 1792–6*. Toronto: Coles Publishing, 1973.

"Red Mulberry (Species at Risk)." Ontario.ca.

"Ginkgo Biloba L." Plants of the World Online.

"Maidenhair Tree or Ginkgo?" CanadianTreeTours.org.

Fraser, Evan E., and W. Andrew Kenney. "Cultural Background and Landscape History as Factors Affecting Perceptions of the Urban Forest." *Journal of Arboriculture* 26, no. 2 (March 2000).

De Sa, Anthony. *Kicking the Sky*. Toronto: Anchor Canada, 2014.

2 • PLANTING SEEDS. THE VICTORIA FRUIT TREE PROJECT

"Gleaning Will Change Our Attitude to Food Waste." Nesta.org.uk.

"The Victoria Fruit Tree Project." Victoria: Victoria Fruit Tree Project, 1998.

Alexander, Christopher, Sara Ishikawa, and Murray
    Silverstein. *A Pattern Language*. New York: Oxford
    University Press, 1977.

Day, Ivan. "Quinces Recipes." HistoricFood.com.

3 • UP A TREE. THE EXPERIENCE

Pollan, Michael. *The Omnivore's Dilemma: A Natural
    History of Four Meals*. New York: Penguin, 2006.

Howard, Alison, and Jessica Brichta. *What's to Eat?
    Improving Food Literacy in Canada*. Report presented
    to the Conference Board of Canada, October 2013.

Jenkins, Patty. "Benefits." TreeClimbing.com.

Tree Climbing Japan official website.

Gathright, John, Yozo Yamada, and Miyako
    Morito. "Tree-Assisted Therapy: Therapeutic
    and Societal Benefits from Purpose-Specific
    Technical Recreational Tree-Climbing Programs."
    Arboriculture & Urban Forestry 34, no. 4 (July 2008).

Selhub, Eva M., and Alan C. Logan. *Your Brain
    on Nature: The Science of Nature's Influence on
    Your Health, Happiness, and Vitality*. Toronto:
    HarperCollins, 2014.

Reich, Lee. "Fruiting Espaliers: A Fusion of Art and
    Science." *Arnoldia* 59, no. 4 (Winter 1999–2000).

"What You Should Know about Fruit Production in
    Ontario." OMAFRA.gov.on.ca.

Masumoto, David Mas. *Epitaph for a Peach: Four Seasons
    on My Family Farm*. New York: Harper One, 2000.

Nelson, Jennifer, and Katherine Zeratsky. "Fruit or
    Vegetable — Do You Know the Difference?"
    Mayo Clinic website. August 15, 2012.
"Nutrition Facts: Most Commonly Consumed Fruits and
    Vegetables in Canada." Canadian Produce Marketing
    Association website.

4 • THE FRUITS OF OUR LABOUR.
SHARING THE BOUNTY

Moll, Jorge, Frank Krueger, Roland Zahn, Matteo
    Pardini, Ricardo de Oliveira-Souza, and Jordan
    Grafman. "Human Fronto-Mesolimbic Networks
    Guide Decisions about Charitable Donation."
    Proceedings of the National Academy of Sciences
    of the United States of America, March 15, 2016.
Saul, Nick, and Andrea Curtis. *The Stop: How the
    Fight for Good Food Transformed a Community
    and Inspired a Movement.* Toronto: Vintage Canada,
    2014.
"Our Story." FoodForSoul.it.
"What Wine Was at the Last Supper?" Vivino website.
    April 10, 2017.

5 • URBAN ORCHARDS. THE COMMUNITY
HEADS BACK OUTSIDE

Gerhold, Henry. "Serviceberry Cultivars Tested as
    Street Trees: Second Report." *Arboriculture and
    Urban Forestry* 34, no. 2 (March 2008).

Harden, Garrett. "The Tragedy of the Commons." 1968.
Accessed February 24, 2016. http://www.garrett
hardinsociety.org/articles/art_tragedy_of_the_
commons.html.

Historic Dartmouth Walking Tour. 2nd ed. Downtown
Dartmouth Business Commission, 2006.

"A Brief History of Zoning Bylaws in Toronto." Toronto
Reference Library blog. December 14, 2015.

Golden, Sheila. "Urban Agriculture Impacts: Social,
Health and Economic: A Literature Review."
University of California Davis. November 13, 2013.

"Urbanization." United Nations Population Fund website.

Reker, Moirika. "Looking for Public Fruits in Finland."
Urban Orchards — Pick Your (City) Fruits (blog).
November 12, 2015.

Clifford, Sue, and Angela King. *The Apple Source Book.*
London: Hodder & Stoughton, 2007.

On page 51, Clifford and King quote from this book:

Crowden, James. *Cider — The Forgotten Miracle.*
Somerton: Cyder Press 2, 1999.

6 • WITHERING ON THE VINE. THE
SLIDE TO FOOD ILLITERACY

Hicks, Kathleen. *Dixie: Orchards to Industry.* Mississauga:
Mississauga Library System, 2006.

Eating Well with Canada's Food Guide. Health Canada, 2011.

Howard, Alison, and Jessica Brichta. *What's to Eat?*

Improving Food Literacy in Canada. Report presented
to the Conference Board of Canada, October 2013.
Series T147-194. Statistics Canada website. Last modi-
fied July 2, 2014.
Obesity Update 2017. OECD.org.

7 • WASSAIL. CELEBRATING
UNDER THE TREES

Bates, Kath. "What Is Wassailing?" Oxford Open
Learning website. December 19, 2016.
Otis, Daniel. "Whitehorse Birds Are Getting Drunk on
Fermented Berries." TheStar.com. November 17,
2014.

CONCLUSION. WAITING FOR SPRING

Harris, Elizabeth. "Instead of Taking Down a Fruit Tree,
Building Around It." *New York Times*, July 30, 2012.
MacLeod, Dan. "Hallelujah! Downed Tree an Answer to
Prayers." *Brooklyn Daily*, August 30, 2011.

HARVEST ORGANIZATIONS

CANADA

There are many harvesters working informally throughout North America and beyond. Each is dependent on volunteer support and charitable donations. Not all work continuously and not all list ongoing contact information. This list represents the long-standing active groups in Canada.

British Columbia
LifeCycles Victoria Fruit Tree Project
Nelson Food Cupboard Harvest Rescue
Okanagan Fruit Tree Project

Vancouver Fruit Tree Project Society

Alberta
Calgary Harvest
Operation Fruit Rescue, Edmonton

Saskatchewan
Out of Your Tree in Saskatoon

Manitoba
Fruit Share Brandon
Fruit Share (Winnipeg and beyond)

Ontario
Appleseed Collective (Transition Guelph)
Fruit Share Barrie
Gleaners Guild (Waterloo Region)
Hamilton Fruit Tree Project
Hidden Harvest (Ottawa)
Not Far From The Tree (Toronto)
Sudbury Shared Harvest

Quebec
Les fruits défendus (Montreal)

Nova Scotia
Found Forgotten Food (Halifax and beyond)

UNITED STATES OF AMERICA

Village Harvest in Northern California includes a directory of about 40 American gleaning organizations on its website.